Spreading Resiliency

Making It Happen for Schools and Communities

Mike M. Milstein
Doris Annie Henry

CORWIN PRESS, INC.
A Sage Publications Company
Thousand Oaks, California

Copyright © 2000 by Corwin Press, Inc.

For information:

Corwin Press, Inc.
A Sage Publications Company
2455 Teller Road
Thousand Oaks, California 91320
E-mail: order@corwinpress.com

Sage Publications Ltd.
6 Bonhill Street
London EC2A 4PU
United Kingdom

Sage Publications India Pvt. Ltd.
M-32 Market
Greater Kailash I
New Delhi 110 048 India

Printed in the United States of America

Library of Congress Cataloging-in-Publication Data

Milstein, Mike M.
    Spreading resiliency : Making it happen for schools and communities /
  by Mike M. Milstein, Doris Annie Henry.
      p. cm.
    Includes bibliographical references and index.
    ISBN 0-8039-6740-3 (cloth: acid-free paper)
    ISBN 0-8039-6741-1 (pbk.: acid-free paper)
    1. Community and school—United States. 2. Educational
change—United States. I. Henry, Doris Annie. II. Title.
    LC221 .M554 1999
    371.19—dc21   99-6582

00 01 02 03 04 05 06 7 6 5 4 3 2 1

Editorial Assistant: Julia Parnell
Production Editor: Denise Santoyo
Editorial Assistant: Patricia Zeman
Typesetter/Designer: Marion Warren
Indexer: Teri Greenberg
Cover Designer: Oscar Desierto

Contents

PART I
Basic Concepts

PART III
Making It Happen for Schools & Communities

Tables and Figures

Resource A: Handouts

Foreword

Someone recently sent me a quote that reminded me, "A man of character finds a special attractiveness in difficulty, since it is only by coming to grips with difficulty that he can realize his potentials." I have no idea who said that, but I know the author understood the core of what resiliency is and should be. *Webster's Collegiate Dictionary* (1993) tells us that resilience is "the ability to recover from or adjust easily to misfortune or change." Since we live in a world of constant change and too much misfortune, the need for teaching resilience makes it as basic as the other R's in education. Education is, after all centered on helping children reach their potential and learning how to overcome difficulty.

It has always interested me why some people bend while others break. I suppose I am interested because, like many others, my own story is one of resilience. My academic career marked my movement from being a non-reader, to slow learner, to underachiever, to honor student. I have always credited my progress to the support of parents and teachers and to an incredibly strong streak of stubbornness which has served me well. Understanding why I am stubborn and resist failure at this point in my life becomes a moot question. To put a twist on the old philosophic statement, "I am stubborn, therefore I am successful."

The exercise of will throughout my life has allowed me to forge through the unknown, to stand strong in the winds of change and to exhibit a sense of self-worth even when external circumstances would question my self-confidence. Yet will, by itself, can merely be aggravating to others or even self-destructive. It has to be balanced by flexibility. I once called this paradox "confident humility." Confident humility is the ability to believe in yourself while leaving room for the possibility that someone else has a better idea. I think the sense of balance implied by this paradox is a key to unlocking our understanding of resiliency. The healthiest place is between the extremes. If you lean too far in one direction, it's easy to be pushed over. A sense of balance allows you to recover and to adjust.

How can schools build the strong, healthy ego implied by that sense of balance? In the wake of the Columbine tragedy, that question becomes even more pertinent and powerful. How can we help our children grow up, unscarred and unscathed, in a changing and disconnected world where images of violence permeate? How can we give children a sense of purpose, a sense of confidence, and a sense of balance when everything around them seems to question purpose, to destroy confidence, and to knock them down before they even get started?

The power of teaching resilience is the power of giving children the strength to handle change and to recover easily from misfortune. Sadly, for many of our children, misfortune is a way of life. How can we, as adults, prepare students for what they need to be resilient people? That is what this book is all about.

Hillary Rodham Clinton wrote a book a few years ago and took the title from an African proverb: "It takes a village to raise a child." This recognizes that the creation of resilient children is not something that is done only in a home or in isolation. It requires a team. Sadly, in today's world we must ask: If it takes a village to raise a child, what does it take to raise a village? Far too many of our children are growing up in a world where there is no village—no safety net of support to catch them when they fall. They are growing up isolated and emotionally neglected. Their emotional care and feeding is being left up to the schools. And far too often, the schools are not up to it. Schools cannot be parent, friend, mentor, guide, doctor, nurse, social worker, and minister. The task is too overwhelming. It does take the village.

A national movement is needed to bind school, family, and community together. The movement toward "schools of promise," which grew out of the America's Promise initiative led by General Colin Powell, is one way of connecting schools to communities. The initiative is rooted in the reality that schools exist at the physical and psychological centers of what can become the village. By helping schools reach out to the community, and the community to reach in to the schools, we can begin building villages around our children.

This effort must be done with a sense of respect and mutuality. There is another proverb less well known but just as appropriate. It reminds us that "when elephants fight, the grass gets trampled." When adults fight, children suffer. Resilience in children starts with adults acting responsibly and respectfully toward each other. Resiliency doesn't just happen; it is created by caring adults. If we expect children to show respect, they must be shown respect, and they must witness it in the adults they observe. That, too, is what this book is about.

Researchers at the University of Minnesota have recently established that a strong connection to schools reduces the risk-taking behaviors that lead to failure. School connection also enhances those behaviors that lead to success. This provides clues to what we must do to create resilient young people. We must find ways to get them connected to school. Caring adults must create a web of support around children for them to grow with a sense of efficacy, which becomes the foundation for resilient behavior. Schools are there to elevate a child's chances for success. The key is the child's ability to stay balanced and to adjust to life's challenges. This can be taught.

Mike Milstein and Annie Henry have given us a blueprint to create schools and communities that will spread resiliency in young people. The book is a guide for making schools and communities healthier places, and it shows how to create an environment that will produce healthier adults and children. Much has been written lately about the school reform movement. I think the movement breaks down because it is, at its core, mechanistic. Even the language of reform uses mechanistic phrases, with much talk of "fixing" and "leveraging." Schools and their communities are essentially organic. They cannot be broken into parts, they must be treated systemically. They do not need fixing, they need healing. This is what the authors contend, and the bulk of the book is about how this can be done. It is not merely a call to action, but a primer for making it happen.

Spreading Resiliency: Making It Happen for Schools and Communities can help school and community leaders create caring places where families and children can move from coping to thriving. Rubber bands are resilient. But their resilience is more than just snapping back into place once they are pulled. They store and release kinetic energy. As any teacher knows, rubber bands are good at propelling small objects. If we are to give our children the gift of success, we must find ways of helping them prosper in an uncertain, and too often unfriendly, environment. We want children to snap back, to recover, and to adjust. We also want them to move forward, to propel themselves with the confident humility that will lead to their success. Through their success, we want them to blaze a trail for all of us. Ultimately, this is what the book is about.

PAUL D. HOUSTON
Executive Director
American Association of School Administrators

Preface

I am because we are.

—A saying of the Xhosa people (South Africa)

Spreading Resiliency is dedicated to helping readers respond to school and community problems in ways that promote the well-being of all community members, regardless of age, ethnicity, or socioeconomic status. We believe that it is urgent to focus attention and energy on this goal. In fact, many community development initiatives are being made across the country in support of this goal. These efforts, some of which are described within the book, provide assurance that there is growing awareness of the need to come to grips with issues and develop responses that can improve the health of our communities.

There are no pat answers when it comes to responding to the complex and significant challenges that confront those who are ready and dedicated to improving the wellness of their schools and communities. But there is enough evidence from efforts currently being conducted around the country to show that schools and communities, working together, *can* begin to shift the emphasis from pathology and fatalism to wellness and support *for everyone!* What is needed is recognition that we *can*, with belief, will, and effort, make a positive difference in the well-being and effectiveness of our schools and communities. Where there is widespread concern and understanding, and where there is vision that is shared by like-minded people, anything is possible.

> The only thing we have to fear is fear itself.
>
> —*Franklin Delano Roosevelt*

Spreading Resiliency is intended to be of help to anyone who is concerned about the well-being of our schools and communities. This includes teachers, administrators, counselors, and other educators; parents and other community members; and leaders of voluntary organizations, higher education institutions, businesses, organizations, and local government agencies. It is presented in workbook style so readers can use it to serve their particular needs and interests. Because every school-community situation is unique, responses must also be unique.

One thing is certain: Moving schools and communities toward resiliency, or better states of wellness and effectiveness, requires that everyone's involvement needs to be encouraged! In fact, involvement is the key to the process. As the ancient Chinese proverb reminds us,

I hear and I forget.
I see and I remember.
I do and I understand.

Organization of the Book

Spreading Resiliency is intended to help everyone become more resilient, but it is not enough to say to individuals, "Learn to be tougher, be more capable, cope better," as long as the environments in which they exist deplete their resiliency capabilities. For this reason, *Spreading Resiliency* is dedicated to helping you learn how to modify environments—classrooms, schools, and communities—in ways that move away from resiliency depletion and toward resiliency building.

In the process, you will be challenged to examine your biases, perceptions, attitudes, and beliefs, all of which directly affect how you see your environment and how you react to it. You may find it challenging to reconceptualize how you view your school and community, but we think you will find it to be worthwhile.

> All our knowledge has its origins in our perceptions.
>
> —Leonardo da Vinci

Spreading Resiliency is organized with emphasis on the concept of community. Part I, which includes the first two chapters, explores the meaning of resiliency and why it is so important for school and community well-being. Chapter 1 presents basic information about resiliency and provides necessary definitions and language systems that will be used throughout the book. Chapter 2 explores the concept of community, which is illusive, partly because of our tendency to move about so frequently and widely and partly because of the rapidly changing demographic composition in many of our communities. We believe that the meaning of community may be undergoing a significant change: Physical proximity is becoming less relevant as the defining basis for community. In fact, community can be defined as an attitude as well as a location.

> Change your thoughts and you change your world.
>
> —Norman Vincent Peale

Part II, which includes four chapters, gets into specific issues and strategies related to promoting resiliency for students, educators, schools, and communities. Chapter 3 focuses on students, their strengths and needs, and how schools can help build their resiliency capacities. We emphasize how schools tend to limit their resiliency-building roles and what they can do to change this situation. Chapter 4 examines the resiliency of educators, their capabilities and difficulties, and how the environments in which they work affect them. Ways that schools can help educators enhance their own resiliency, and, in the process, help them to be better role models for their students are examined. Chapter 5 explores how schools and school districts can either detract from or support the resiliency needs of students, educators, and community members. With some forethought, there are ways that schools and school districts can be organized, structured, and operated to be more supportive. Chapter 6 focuses on the basic elements of school communities. Communities are vitally important to the support and maintenance of our schools. Schools need to learn how to partner better with their communities so they can provide effective education for students. We also believe that schools need to take responsibility for supporting and sustaining their surrounding communities. The chapter examines ways that schools can become more proactive as partners with their communities.

Part III presents strategies to help schools and communities bring their resources together in ways that support resiliency initiatives and provides examples of communities that are currently engaged in this important work. Chapter 7 offers suggestions for facilitating the introduction of resiliency in schools and communities. The emphasis is on concepts and skills required to manage and assess change. Chapter 8 gives descriptions of some of the efforts under way in communities around the country that are, in one way or another, aimed at the development of resilient schools and communities. Reading about these efforts can be quite helpful to those who are interested in trying to improve resiliency in their schools and communities. For those who may be interested, basic information, including ways of making contact, is provided for these and other community resiliency initiatives. Last, resources that can be used to guide school and community resiliency efforts are catalogued.

Spreading Resiliency is a highly interactive book. There are activities throughout the first six chapters that can help you develop a better understanding of the concepts and strategies presented. Included are ways of diagnosing current situations and selecting strategies for change, as well as questions, exercises, surveys, quotations, and other stimuli that are intended to help members of your school and community dialogue and, hopefully, engage in challenging activities that can, literally, spread resiliency. To promote this purpose, we strongly encourage you to pursue the activities that are suggested in the book. Furthermore, to the extent that you are able to engage others, it may turn out to be the start of a journey toward the development of a healthier, more resilient school and community!

We have not suggested time frames for the exercises because each situation is different (e.g., number of individuals involved, time available, and readiness to engage), which can vary from low interest, to concern, to commitment to take whatever steps are necessary to promote resiliency in the school and in the community. Depending on the situation, the exercises can be used for a variety of purposes, ranging from awareness raising at short meetings to in-depth focus at retreats dedicated to goal setting and action planning. If people are ready to engage, the more time that is committed, the more comprehensive the discussion will be and the more likely it is that shared understandings and commitments will be developed.

Last, we would like to give thanks to the many educators and community members whose input has helped us advance our thinking about resilient schools and communities. The collaboration between Nan Henderson and Mike Milstein (1996), which resulted in the publication of *Resiliency in Schools: Making It Happen for Students and Educators,* provided the basic framework for the understanding and further development of our work on resiliency. Our presentations at educator conferences, as well as the numerous workshops we have conducted in school districts across the country, have provided important feedback that has led to modifications in our thinking. Our work with the Ashland, Oregon, community in pursuing community resiliency, which is summarized in Chapter 8, provided the initial stimulus for the development of the book. In particular, Dr. John Daggett, Superintendent of the Ashland Public Schools, provided the vision and leadership required to make the Ashland dream a reality and encouraged us to continue our efforts regarding community resiliency. To all these wonderful people who have shared their thoughts and efforts with us so openly and freely, we give our heartfelt thanks. The contributions of the following reviewers are also gratefully acknowledged:

Sandra L. Stacki
Hofstra University, Hempstead, NY

Mary Ann Sweet
School Counselor
Tomball Elementary School, Tomball, TX

Kathryn LeLaurin
Family Learning Foundation, Inc.
Memphis, TN

Judith Olsen
Instructional Services Consultant
Lakeland Area Education Agency 3, Cylinder, IA

We hope that you find resiliency as an approach to school and community improvement as exciting and important as we do. If you engage in efforts aimed at supporting the resiliency of your community and its members, we would appreciate hearing about your efforts.

Mike M. Milstein
D. Annie Henry
The Resiliency Group, Ltd.
4520 Compound Ct. NW
Albuquerque, NM 87107

About the Authors

Mike M. Milstein is a partner in The Resiliency Group, Ltd., and Professor of Educational Leadership at the University of New Mexico. His teaching, research, and writing interests are in the areas of resiliency and organizational change and development. He has been actively engaged in school and community resiliency development efforts in such places as Ashland, Oregon; Battle Creek, Michigan; and Shelby County, Tennessee. The resiliency initiatives he has facilitated include classroom instruction and curriculum improvement efforts, schoolwide activities that enhance the resiliency of educators, and school-community partnerships that support resiliency development for both children and adults. He has written 11 books, including coauthoring *Resiliency in Schools* (1996).

Doris "Annie" Henry is a partner in The Resiliency Group, Ltd., and Professor of Educational Leadership at New Mexico Highlands University. Her research and writing interests focus on resiliency, restructuring, change, organization development, and school improvement. Her work with developing resiliency efforts includes Ashland, Oregon; Tennessee State Department of Education; and Memphis, Tennessee. She has facilitated resiliency at the classroom, schoolwide, and community-school partnership levels. Her professional career includes being Professor of Educational Leadership at the University of Memphis and at the University of Nebraska at Omaha, an elementary school principal for nearly a decade in Arizona and Oklahoma, and a classroom teacher. She has published widely in her areas of interest, most notably as coauthor of the national study, *Becoming a Superintendent: Challenges of School District Leadership* (1997).

PART I

Basic Concepts

CHAPTER 1

Resiliency

Promoting Success for Everyone

It's a funny thing about life. If you refuse to accept anything but the best, you very often get it.

—Somerset Maugham

These are trying times for schools and communities. It is during such times that schools, families, and communities need to come together to provide mutual support and improve the potential for *everyone*—youngsters, adults, and the elderly—to lead positive, meaningful, and healthy lives.

For this to happen, we need to focus on our problems and how we can change and improve the situation. This chapter explores underlying problems and the urgency for more effective school and community responses to these problems. It also provides an introduction to resiliency, which is an important and positive shift in the way we think about and respond to our school and community environments. Fostering resiliency in classrooms, schools, school districts, families, volunteer groups and organizations, and formal governmental agencies can do much to move us along the path to school and community improvement.

Why the Urgency?

Many school districts are challenged by a rising tide of problems that include gang-related activities, substance abuse, absenteeism, high dropout rates, students with minimal English proficiency, decreasing parental involvement and support, and changing family structures. Communities are also being challenged by problems such as a growing number of its members unable to maintain a decent quality of life, a growing disparity between the haves and the have-nots, a fracturing of acceptance and trust among individuals and groups, a declining level of participation in civic affairs, and, in general, a growing distrust of government's intentions or abilities to function equitably and effectively on behalf of all citizens. Exercise 1.1 can help give you a picture of how your community is doing with these issues.

EXERCISE 1.1. Taking Stock of School and Community Problems

To what extent are the school and community problems, identified at the outset of this chapter, realities in your own community?

An important initial step in making significant change is to be sure that everyone understands and agrees about the current state of affairs. Invite others to respond to the question with you. Remember to focus on perceptions about what the situation is *now*. Follow-up questions for the group to explore might include the following:

1. What problems do you think are being encountered by the schools in your community that hinder their ability to provide effective education for students?
2. What problems do you think are being encountered by the community that hinders its ability to provide support needed by its members?
3. Why do you think your school and community are experiencing these problems?
4. Are any of these problems being addressed? If so, in what ways?

Record members' responses to these questions on a chalkboard or on a sheet of chart paper. Ask the group to review the responses and identify shared beliefs. Underline agreements or rewrite those that might need to be modified so they can serve as the basis for further discussion if the group agrees to continue the conversation, as well as for actions if the group decides to pursue ways of spreading resiliency.

> We live in the midst of alarms; anxiety beclouds the future; we expect some new disaster with each newspaper we read.
>
> —Abraham Lincoln

Living in stressful times is extremely challenging. We are not the first, nor will we be the last, to feel the pressures of stressful times.

Still, although life has always been accompanied by challenges, this reality has been especially true during the closing decades of the 20th century because of the pace of change that has been experienced. Accompanying the rapidity of change are breakdowns of institutions such as the church and the family, which have traditionally acted as sources of shared understanding, support, and authority for communities, nations, and the world.

With these breakdowns have come an endless array of problems that appear to be intractable.

For Children and Adolescents

We are all too familiar with the many negative manifestations that are exhibited by children and adolescents in these trying times. These include

- Various forms of antisocial behavior, such as vandalism and truancy
- Negative peer influence, including antisocial gang membership
- Violence and crime
- Broken families
- Child abuse
- Drug abuse
- High unemployment rates among teens
- Academic failure and school dropouts
- Premarital teen births
- Hopelessness

Add other factors that you think are important:

- _____
  _____
- _____
  _____
- _____
  _____

For Schools

Schools, whether rural, small-town, suburban, or urban, are confronted with major challenges, many of which test our limited abilities to create effective responses, including

- Fear and violence
- Increasing student enrollments and, often, larger class sizes
- Unionization and collective bargaining
- An aging workforce
- Dilapidated buildings
- Technological breakthroughs
- Decreasing parental and community involvement

Add other factors that you think are important:

- _____
  _____
- _____
  _____
- _____
  _____

For Families

A major factor in the increasing rates of youth problems is the breakdown occurring in traditional family structures. For example, there are wide-spread occurrences of

- Marital problems and high divorce rates
- Single-parent families
- Absence of extended families
- Families with no adult members available during the day, which has exacerbated the growing problems associated with the latchkey children phenomenon
- Negative adult role modeling regarding addictive behaviors associated with tobacco, alcohol, and other drugs
- Lack of clarity about family roles and responsibilities
- Lack of close family and friendship ties
- Lack of motivation for achievement

Add other factors that you think are important:

- _____
  _____
- _____
  _____
- _____
  _____

For Communities

Communities provide the frame of reference, the basic orientation that guides all members' behaviors, whether they are children, adolescents, or adults. Communities will be hard pressed to provide the positive guidance that is necessary, unless adequate responses are developed regarding problems such as the following:

- High mobility rates and their affect on members' attachments to communities

- Inequities in earning and housing opportunities
- Lack of challenging employment opportunities
- Fragmentation of values and norms
- Fear and violence
- Lack of opportunities to gather, interact, and celebrate

Add other factors that you think are important:

- _____
  _____
- _____
  _____
- _____
  _____

The problems listed are just the tip of the iceberg. They can easily be extended. The old Chinese curse, "You should live in interesting times," certainly applies to the current reality in most of the communities in which we live. One perspective is that what we are witnessing is a community structure that is coming apart at the seams. Another perspective, which is less pessimistic, is that we are living through a major transition that may be confusing, disorienting, and erratic but one that is also natural, necessary, and responsive to changing times.

Many problems appear to be intractable, because we focus on them narrowly as student problems, school problems, family problems, or community problems. In reality, they are interconnected and affect each other, sometimes positively and sometimes negatively. Figure 1.1 illustrates this basic interconnection.

As Figure 1.1 denotes, each subsystem overlaps the other subsystems. Sometimes, the connections are unilateral, such as when schools deal with

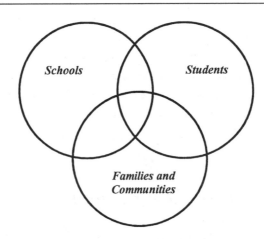

Figure 1.1.   The Linkages Between Students, Schools, and Families-Communities

student-related issues. Sometimes, the connections are multifaceted, such as when communities and families interact with schools and students in the process of education. The important thing to realize is that because they are interconnected and affect each other, it is not likely that working to improve any one of them without making parallel efforts with the others will have a lasting impact. Narrowly focusing on one subsystem does not account for the potential impacts, positive and negative, that can be caused by other subsystems.

We need to develop supportive partnerships across the three subsystems because of their interconnections, which means that problems are frequently shared. Some examples of how the subsystems share the same problems include drug abuse in the schools and in the community, segregated housing and segregated schools, and broken homes and children who exhibit antisocial behaviors in school and in the community. Such problems are not likely to be solved unless our responses are holistic and involve representatives from all three subsystems.

Issues that seem to be unique and limited to any one of the subsystems, such as student learning difficulties, educator stress, school climate, family support for children's' growth and development, or the well-being of the community itself, are in reality more likely to be related and interconnected. Initiating a program here or a project there is not likely to make much of a dent in the problems we observe. To be effective, we need to create comprehensive responses to comprehensive problems, responses that cut across the different subsystems identified in Figure 1.1. Furthermore, these responses should focus on prevention where possible and on early intervention when it is too late for prevention. The absolute worst option is to wait until problems have become full-blown crises. Too often, this is what happens, but it is neither a reasonable nor effective way of responding to complex problems.

> What is the use of a house if you haven't got a tolerable planet to put it on?
>
> —Henry David Thoreau

We are witnessing a major shift toward understanding the connections between schools, families, and communities. We can no longer drift along and hope for the best while preparing for the worst. Rather, we need to work at understanding our problems and formulating positive and effective communitywide structures and processes to respond to them. The fact that you have chosen to read this book indicates that you are probably thinking about joining those who are already participating in this important effort.

The Problem With Problem Solvers

We need to revisit how we think about schools, families, and communities. It is seductively easy to focus on problems, deficits, or at-risk behavior. After all, they are easy enough to find. They are all around us! Furthermore, most of us pride ourselves on being problem solvers, and we all know what problem solvers do—they look for problems to solve! In other words, most of us have *mind maps* that emphasize the shortcomings, the risk behaviors, the difficulties (i.e., the reasons that things *do not, cannot,* or *will not work*). Exercise 1.2 can shed some light on this.

> The essence of belief is the establishment of a habit.
> —*Charles S. Pearce*

EXERCISE 1.2. What You See Is What You Get

This exercise can be done individually, but it will have more lasting effects if it is done in a group.

1. Think about a situation at your school or in your community that seems to be highly resistant to improvement. Select a situation that has meaning for you. Examples might include ineffective discipline policies and procedures, poor academic achievement, low morale among faculty members, low parental involvement, high crime rates, or community apathy.
2. List all the reasons why things don't or can't work regarding the situation you selected. Put them on a chalkboard or on a sheet of chart paper. You probably can list many reasons why things don't or can't work. In fact, the list probably looks quite imposing.
3. Now, regarding the same situation, think of all the reasons why things work as well as they work now. In other words, things could probably be worse. Why aren't they? What positive things are going on? Record these reasons on a chalkboard or on a sheet of chart paper.
4. What other practical things can be done to improve the situation? Record these suggestions.
5. Was your response to the fourth question less than enthusiastic? Do you think that the situation is intractable?
6. Or does the situation seem less difficult or negative now that you have given some thought to the positive side of it?

If you found it difficult to see the positive side of the situation and the potential for its improvement, you may be exhibiting the approach of the "dreaded problem solver" who finds it easier to focus on the "can'ts" and "won'ts" than the "cans" and "wills." Problem solvers readily identify deficits, but this focus can also leave them less sensitive to the identification of assets.

> Is the unspoken worldview that underlies the assumptions from which I practice my profession perhaps, unwittingly, contributing to the very problems that I am committed to solve?
> —*Anne Wilson Schaef*

Problem-solver thinking can best be described as a pathology-focused approach because it focuses on behavioral difficulties, such as teen pregnancy, school dropouts, drug abuse, and criminal behavior. Focusing on behavioral difficulties, problem solvers look for patterns, such as broken homes, dysfunctional neighborhoods, and poverty, to explain these behaviors.

They assume that individuals whose demographics resemble those of others who exhibit such problem behaviors will probably begin to exhibit similar behaviors at some point in time. Problem solvers then plan and act accordingly. In short, problem solvers are likely to see problems even where they may not exist.

Equally troublesome, problem solvers may also fail to see strengths that are right in front of them because they are so busy focusing on problems! Worst of all, where predispositions lead us to anticipate certain behaviors, the Pygmalion effect is likely to take effect as we label individuals and groups, whether negatively or positively! That is, people will behave according to our expectations.

As Covey (1989) notes,

Whether they shift us in positive or negative directions, whether they are instantaneous or developmental, paradigm shifts move us from one way of seeing the world to another. And those shifts create powerful change. Our paradigms, correct or incorrect, are the sources of our attitudes and behaviors and ultimately our relationships with others. (p. 30)

> The hopeful man sees success where others see failure, sunshine where others see shadows and storm.
>
> —O. S. Marden

What is needed is nothing less than a radical shift in how we think about youngsters, schools, and communities. We need to free ourselves of the problem-focused, "can't do" orientation and move on to a wellness-focused, "can do" orientation, because what we see is the best predictor of what we get!

The resiliency approach is a powerful paradigm shift that has the potential of reversing this debilitating mind set. The current shift in perspective from pathology to resiliency is dramatic.

The pathology perspective focuses on maladaptation, deficits, illness, and problems. The resiliency perspective focuses on wellness, adaptation, protective factors, and solutions. It is a mind map that emphasizes the possible, the belief that things can and will work. As Blum's (1998) review of resiliency in *Psychology Today* points out, resiliency represents a way of thinking that is a "breathtaking change" from the problem solver's victim-and-damage focus that was promoted by psychology from the 1940s until quite recently.

> . . . Enhance the humanity of the other, because in that process, you enhance your own.
>
> —Desmond Tutu

Resiliency is about cultivating the capacity to bounce back and grow stronger as a result of life's experiences. Throughout life, each of us has many opportunities to bounce back and become stronger. From prenatal experience until our dying days, there are endless challenges that can foster resiliency, including

- Growing from an embryo to a full birth delivery
- Mastering basic human survival skills, such as walking and communicating

- Expanding connectedness and relationships beyond the family of origin
- Leaving the family of origin and establishing one's own place in the world
- Gaining the knowledge and skills required to be self-supporting
- Taking responsibility for others, including supporting spouses and children and assuming formal leadership roles
- Coping with physical and emotional manifestations of aging
- Reflecting on the meaning of life
- Bringing closure to life

Each of us can easily expand on this bare-bones list of life's challenges, all of which have the potential to promote and enhance resiliency from our own life's experiences. For some, the road through life is paved with endless challenges that are environmentally related, such as poverty, broken homes, drug or other addictions, or lack of adequate support systems. Many do not have to travel such bumpy roads but, for most of us, there are likely to be more than sufficient opportunities to test our resiliency.

> No individual can arrive even at the threshold of his potentialities without a culture in which he participates.
> —*Ruth Benedict*

For those with too many safeguards (e.g., wealth, overprotective parents, security from daily risk) and promises of privileged positions in the future, there may not be sufficient opportunities to develop necessary coping skills and resiliency capabilities. In fact, there may be more danger for those who have too much protection than there is for those who are, often, viewed as at risk.

> Adversity reveals genius, prosperity conceals it.
> —*Horace*

An Introduction to Resiliency

There are a variety of definitions and models of resiliency. For example, resiliency might be viewed as "the process of coping with disruptive, stressful, or challenging life events in a way that provides the individual with additional protective and coping skills than prior to the disruption that results from the event" (Richardson, Neiger, Jensen, & Krumpfer, 1990, p. 34). Similarly, it can be seen as the "process of self-righting and growth" (Higgins, 1994, p. 1) or "the capacity to bounce back, to withstand hardship, and to repair yourself" (Wolin & Wolin, 1993, p. 5). These definitions have much in common—gaining additional protective factors, self-righting, and bouncing back. All have to do with the capacity to meet challenges and become more capable as a result of these experiences.

Our world is changing rapidly. Either we respond effectively to these changes or we become victims of them. Some people collapse or barely survive adversity. Others, the resilient ones, bounce back and become stronger by learning new skills and developing creative ways of coping. They meet life's challenges, overcome them, and use their experiences to improve their abilities to deal with the inevitable problems that will come their way in the future.

What is it about these people that allows them to be so resilient? More important, what can we learn from them to increase our own resiliency? Higgins (1994) believes that resilient individuals have three qualities in common. First, they maintain a positive attitude. Second, they confront issues and take charge of their own lives. Third, and above all else, they have a deep and abiding faith that creates meaning in their lives. These qualities are regularly found among resilient adults, no matter how rocky or smooth their lives have been. Like most important things in life, it calls for effort and the courage to change beliefs and habits. Exercise 1.3 can help you get a picture of your own resiliency (this exercise is available in the Resource section as Handout 1).

EXERCISE 1.3. How Resilient Are You?

How resilient are you? Here's a little test to help you get a sense of your own resiliency. Circle the choice that is most true or typical of you for each of the following questions:

1. When you have difficulties, are you more likely to:
   a. Confront them immediately by taking an initiative
   b. Get away from the difficulties in hopes they will pass
2. What is your attitude toward leisure time?
   a. Enjoy reading, learning, and exploring
   b. Ponder your situation and worry about your future
3. When faced with a challenge, do you:
   a. Enjoy the challenge of figuring out the dilemmas and making things happen
   b. Let others take the lead
4. Are your work and home environments:
   a. Supportive and energizing
   b. Stressful and exhausting
5. Do you believe that:
   a. Good things are most likely to happen to you
   b. Bad things are most likely to happen to you
6. Do you believe that the best years of your life are:
   a. Yet to come
   b. Behind you
7. Do you:
   a. Have a clear sense of purpose about life
   b. Find yourself drifting from year to year without goals
8. How do you feel about your accomplishments and abilities:
   a. Proud of your accomplishments and your abilities
   b. Not as capable as you could be when coping with challenging situations

---

EXERCISE 1.3. Continued

9. When going through life's inevitable transitions, do you:
   a. Feel at ease with them
   b. Feel unsettled and in need of more time to adjust
10. Do you believe that you:
    a. Must earn what you get
    b. Are entitled to rewards that you want

The more "a" responses that you selected, the more likely it is that you exhibit resilient behaviors. These responses indicate that you probably feel good about yourself most of the time and take pride in your accomplishments. You also probably take challenges that come your way as a part of life and work hard to respond to them effectively.

If you chose "b" responses more than "a" responses, you might want to consider making some changes.

First, you may want to work on changing your attitude and behaviors by practicing more positive self-talk, especially if you tend to be critical of yourself.

Second, you may want to observe and talk with people you think are highly resilient to see what you can learn from them.

Third, you may want to read and think about resiliency-related areas, such as self-esteem, career development, life stages, and dealing with transitions.

In whatever ways possible, try to learn about and practice the qualities and skills that promote resiliency.

Internal and Environmental Protective Factors

What are the basic factors that make up resiliency? One way of categorizing them is to think of those things that are *internal* to individuals and those things that are *external* to individuals, or within their environments. Table 1.1 identifies key internal and environmental protective factors that are needed for the development and maintenance of resiliency. (It's Handout 2 in the Resource section.)

Exercise 1.4, which follows, is intended to help you gain a better sense of your own internal and environmental protective factors.

> With a good heredity, nature deals you a fine hand at cards; and with a good environment, you learn to play the hand well.
>
> —*Walter C. Alvarez*

The extent to which we exhibit resiliency is directly related to the extent to which the internal and environmental protective factors identified in Table 1.1 exist in our lives. Most important, as the ideas and strategies presented in the book illustrate, there is much that we can do to promote these factors for everyone, both children and adults, in our communities.

TABLE 1.1   Internal and Environmental Protective Factors

Internal Protective Factors
Characteristics of Individuals That Promote Resiliency

1. Gives of self in service to others or a cause or both
2. Uses life skills, including good decision making, assertiveness, impulse control, and problem solving
3. Is sociable and has ability to be a friend and form positive relationships
4. Has a sense of humor
5. Exhibits internal locus of control (i.e., belief in ability to influence one's environment)
6. Is autonomous, independent
7. Has positive view of personal future
8. Is flexible
9. Has spirituality (i.e., belief in a greater power)
10. Has capacity for connection to learning
11. Is self-motivated
12. Is "good at something," has personal competence
13. Has feelings of self-worth and self-confidence
14. Other:

Environmental Protective Factors
Characteristics Modeled by Families, Schools,
Communities, and Peer Groups that Promote Resiliency

1. Promotes close bonds
2. Values and encourages education
3. Uses high warmth, low criticism style of interaction
4. Sets and enforces clear boundaries (rules, norms, and laws)
5. Encourages supportive relationships with many caring others
6. Promotes sharing of responsibilities, service to others, "required helpfulness"
7. Provides access to resources for meeting basic needs of housing, employment, health care, and recreation
8. Expresses high and realistic expectations for success
9. Encourages goal setting and mastery
10. Encourages prosocial development of values (such as altruism) and life skills (such as cooperation)
11. Provides leadership, decision making, and other opportunities for meaningful participation
12. Appreciates the unique talents of each individual
13. Other:

SOURCE: Adapted from Henderson and Milstein (1996).

EXERCISE 1.4. Your Resiliency Story

Exercise 1.4 is intended to give you and other members of your group a chance to become more familiar with the internal and environmental protective factors listed on Table 1.1. As you become more aware of these factors, you will find it easier to observe and assess the extent to which you and others in your school and community, both children and adults, exhibit them.

1. Think about a time in your life that was especially challenging or difficult (e.g., death of a loved one, a divorce, a financial crisis, or major physical problems).
2. Review the list of internal protective factors in Table 1.1 (or Handout 2). Which of these were you able to draw on to help you through this difficult situation? If there are other internal protective factors you think are important, add them to the list.
3. Review the list of environmental protective factors. Which of these were you able to draw on? If there are other environmental protective factors that you think are important, add them to the list.
4. What other internal and environmental factors listed in Table 1.1 do you think would have been helpful to get you through the situation?
5. Share your life situation and your internal and environmental protective factors assessment with others and ask them to share theirs with you.

Resiliency Factors

A different way of structuring our thinking about resiliency is to summarize the key findings of the at risk literature (e.g., Hawkins, Catalano, & Miller, 1992) and the resiliency literature (e.g., Benard, 1991; Werner & Smith, 1992) into factors, as depicted in Figure 1.2.

As the resiliency wheel (Henderson & Milstein, 1996) depicts, there are six key factors that make up resiliency: (a) prosocial bonding, (b) clear and consistent boundaries, (c) life skills, (d) caring and support, (e) high expectations, and (f) meaningful participation. Whether referring to children or adults, schools or communities, these factors are the basic building blocks of resiliency. They can be defined as follows:

1. Prosocial bonding: Connections with persons and activities that are healthy and supportive of positive growth and development. Those with strong prosocial bonds that emphasize healthy relationships and behaviors are less likely to engage in risk-related relationships and behaviors.

He who has a why to live can bear almost any how.
—*Friedrich Nietzsche*

2. Clear and consistent boundaries: Defined and agreed-on expectations for behavior, along with appropriate consequences that are enforced regularly and equitably. Clear and consistent boundaries can lead to feelings of safety and freedom, and in turn, to more positive participation.

To enjoy freedom we have to control ourselves.
—*Virginia Woolf*

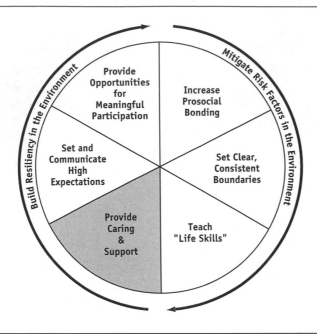

Figure 1.2. The Resiliency Wheel

The supreme end of education is expert discernment in all things—the power to tell the good from the bad, the genuine from the counterfeit.
—Samuel Johnson

3. Life skills: Communications, problem solving, decision making, planning, goal setting, cooperation, healthy conflict resolution, and assertiveness. These are skills that are required to successfully navigate life.

The deepest principle of Human Nature is the craving to be appreciated.
—William James

4. Caring and support: Unconditional positive regard, encouragement, trust, and love. Caring and support can lead to an increased sense of worth and value.

Lord, grant that I may always desire more than I can accomplish.
—Michelangelo

5. High expectations: Achievement orientation that is based on abilities and potential provides motivation. High but realistic expectations support success.

Few things help an individual more than to place responsibility on him, and to let him know that you trust him.
—Booker T. Washington

6. Meaningful participation: Opportunities to become involved; help others; engage in group problem solving, decision making, planning, and goal setting. Meaningful participation can promote belonging and connection.

Now, take a look at Exercise 1.5.

By now, it should be apparent that although resiliency may be a relatively new term to you, the basic factors are deeply embedded in your own life. We all give daily attention to coping and succeeding, and as we do so,

---

EXERCISE 1.5. You and the Resiliency Wheel

This exercise is intended to help you become more acquainted and comfortable with the six resiliency factors just described. It should also help you establish a sense of your own resiliency status and ways that you contribute to the resiliency of others.

1. Review the definitions for each of the six resiliency factors. Identify and record the extent to which they actually exist and promote resiliency in your own life situation.

   - Prosocial bonding:

   - Clear and consistent boundaries:

   - Life skills:

   - Caring and support:

   - High expectations:

   - Meaningful participation:

2. Share your thoughts about the extent to which each factor exists in your life with other individuals, and ask them to do the same with you.
3. Now, think about ways you promote the resiliency of others you know and care about, particularly your friends and family members. Describe how you try to provide support for each of the resiliency factors for these individuals.

   - Prosocial bonding:

   - Clear and consistent boundaries:

   - Life skills:

   - Caring and support:

   - High expectations:

   - Meaningful participation:

4. Share your list with others and ask them to do the same with you.

EXERCISE 1.5. Continued

5. Last, discuss responses to the following questions with others.
   - Were you able to identify many things that support your resiliency?

     _____

   - Were you able to identify many things you do to support the resiliency of others you care about?

     _____

   - Was your list similar to those of other participants?

     _____

   - Did you find it easier to list thoughts for some of the six factors than you did for others regarding yourself? Regarding others?

     _____

   - If so, why do you think this is the situation?

     _____

> Experience is not what happens to a man; it is what a man does with what happens to him.
> —*Aldous Huxley*

> Life is a series of experiences, each one of which makes us bigger, even though sometimes it is hard to realize this.
> —*Henry Ford*

> The world breaks everyone and afterward some are stronger in the broken places
> —*Ernest Hemingway*

we enhance our own resiliency. We seek situations that provide opportunities for us to charge our resiliency batteries as well as opportunities to help others charge theirs. In like manner, we instinctively shield ourselves from situations that are negative and can drain our resiliency batteries.

As Table 1.1 makes clear, resiliency is not just about developing individual capabilities. It is also about developing resiliency-supporting environments. There is a direct relationship between how supportive our environments are and how resilient we feel and behave. For instance, very few of those who survived the Holocaust during World War II emerged from that experience as whole, healthy individuals. The Holocaust is an extreme case of an environment that purposefully and comprehensively depleted the resiliency of those who were caught up in it. Fortunately, few of us have been put to such a severe test.

Still, we do live in trying times marked by rapidly changing societal conditions. Our ability to respond effectively to these conditions, as individuals, groups, and communities, is a major challenge. Our willingness and competence to meet the challenges will dictate how effective we will be in positively affecting the resiliency of ourselves, those we are responsible for and care about, our schools and communities and ultimately, the long-term well-being of our country and our world.

How do we begin to meet the challenge? How do we come to an agreed-on understanding of the situation and what needs to be done to improve it? As a start, Chapter 2 provides a frame of reference that is intended to help readers gain clarity about the concept of community and the importance of fostering resiliency in their own communities.

CHAPTER 2

Resilient Communities

What Are They?

It is only in our relationships with others that we are clearly able to see ourselves.
—Hesselbein, Goldsmith, Beckhard,
and Schubert (1998, p. xii)

When we talk and think about communities, it feels as natural as apple pie. But when asked to describe our communities, our experiences and our interactions bound our responses. Our schools, places of worship, workplaces, housing subdivision, shopping areas, and parks are all part of the community portrait.

Whatever it is called and however it is defined, it is the place that each of us is connected to in some way. In fact, communities are about connections. This chapter explores the relationship of the ecology of the community to its members' wellness or resiliency. For schools and their communities to connect and interact in ways that are healthy, it is important to explore and define the concept of community.

The intent of the chapter is to help the reader gain a clearer sense of what a community is and what is needed for it to respond to members' needs in healthy and resilient ways. Relationships in communities are explored to gain a better understanding of how they can form the essential components of community building. To accomplish this, the chapter has been divided into five sections. First, understanding why community development and building resiliency are important is addressed. Second, traditional ways of thinking about community are examined. This is followed by exploration of the shifting realities of communities, and then by ways of visualizing a resilient community. Last, a foundation for building a resilient community is developed.

Further discussion on exploring community resiliency is dealt with in the last three chapters of the book. Chapter 6 goes into more detail on issues and possibilities for improving the resiliency of communities. Chapter 7 focuses on managing and assessing change, and Chapter 8 presents examples of communities that are becoming more resilient and healthy.

Why Community Development and Building Resiliency Are Important

Belonging to a community means belonging to something that is larger than one's self. A healthy community is characterized by

- Members' sense of belonging
- Shared values and beliefs
- An infrastructure that supports well-being
- Common goals that benefit everyone

> I am more convinced than ever of the importance of reinventing community, both within our schools and within our neighborhoods. This sense of place, of belonging, is a crucial building block for the healthy development of children and adolescents.
>
> —James Comer

Healthy communities meet challenges in constructive and resilient ways. Challenges cause them to grow stronger. One of the prevalent problems that is detrimental to the continuous well-being of any community is the failure to ensure the inclusion of all voices. Typically, there is a small core of people who willingly and actively give in ways that help the community. They may be small in numbers, but they are the ones who are motivated to make a difference and are willing to expend the energy that is required. They are almost always there, and we are thankful they are.

> No individual can arrive even at the threshold of his potentialities without a culture in which he participates. Conversely, no civilization has in it any element which in the last analysis is not the contribution of an individual.
>
> —Ruth Benedict

The challenge is to expand participation to include other stakeholders in the community so that they can express their values and beliefs and join others to move the community in positive, constructive ways. For community resiliency to be developed, members have to have a sense of belonging. There has to be involvement across *all* segments of the population.

It is relatively simple to reach out to the ones who are easily accessible. Their skills and abilities are already known, and they have proven themselves to be responsive. Others who have the same values and beliefs and

> The history of man is a graveyard of great cultures that came to catastrophic ends because of their incapacity for planned, rational, voluntary reaction to challenge.
>
> —Erich Fromm

are in the same approximate physical location also need to come together in positive, constructive ways. But do we know who they are? If we do, do we welcome them? Reaching these other voices in the community takes effort, time, and planning. Without this effort, there will be perceptions of exclusion, which can fracture the community further and swell the number of members who feel disaffected.

One Community at a Time

Every community must take its own path to resiliency. Take, for example, the comments of a Native American from Alaska who reflected on the problems his Arctic Circle village was having with child abuse, alcoholism, gambling, malnutrition, and violence: "They took away the people one by one for treatment, but really the disease was in the village. We could only understand what was happening by looking at the community" (Pipher, 1996, p. 15).

Communities can provide for the basic human need to relate and connect. We all need interactions with familiar, supportive people on a regular basis. Relationships are essential to our well-being and growth. Without healthy relationships, individuals merely survive or possibly become dysfunctional. If we help each other to survive and learn from the experience, we improve and become more resilient as individuals and as a community.

> The health of a democratic society may be measured by the quality of functions performed by private citizens.
>
> —Alexis de Tocqueville

Resilient communities are those that use challenges to become healthier. Because no two communities are alike, knowing the individuals and groups within our communities, having a collective sense of purpose, and promoting relationships that are healthy is a good starting place to encourage resiliency.

Traditional Ways of Thinking About Community

Everyone has stories about the community they know best, the one in which they grew up. These early images of community are firmly planted in our minds. Exercise 2.1 is intended to help clarify the meaning of community by encouraging you to delve into yours from your youth as well as the one you're in now.

EXERCISE 2.1. If You Don't Know Where You Are, How Can You Know Where You Are Going?

This exercise is intended to give you a better sense of your own history of community and to give you and your group a clearer understanding of the community in which you live, and probably work in, now. It can help identify ways of moving the community in which you live and work to a healthier place.

Think about the community in which you grew up. How would you describe it? What were its strong points? What were the shortcomings? This exercise works best in dyads or in small groups.

1. Take 2 or 3 minutes to reflect on the community in which you grew up. Jot down the strengths of that community and the areas you would have liked to change.
2. Have each person share the strengths and areas to change with others in your group or dyad.
3. After everyone is finished, make two columns on chart paper or a chalkboard: strengths and shortcomings. Record everyone's strengths and shortcomings. Identify the commonalities.
4. Community has meaning for individuals as well as for groups. What are some common ways group members define their communities? Record agreements.
5. Last, ask members to compare the communities in which they grew up with the ones in which they are living or working (or both) in now:
   • How are they similar? How are they different?
   • What can you learn from the community in which you grew up that may be beneficial to the community you are in presently?
   • Challenge the group to craft a meaningful definition of community.

Shifting Realities of Community: From Rural to Urban and Suburban

The community that many of us desire is one that is captured by images of places in the past when agrarian life predominated. For the most part, images we hold are of caring and positive relationships. They also include a clear sense of geographic boundaries, widespread support for economic and community development, familiarity, and a common set of values about how we all benefit from being a part of a community.

> Man shapes himself through decisions that shape his environment.
> —Rene Dubos

Rural Communities

Our American rural heritage is perceived as one in which community members shared values and where lives were shaped by shared economic development. Geographically, communities were separated from each other, but within them, people lived close to each other. In many instances, just about everyone in the community was known. Similar to many tribal or clan cultures, communities were territorial, bounded by proximity.

We tend to romanticize the rural or small town setting. Certainly, it has exhibited strengths. It is a place where every-one is known, and it is small enough to pro-mote togetherness and support, belonging and protection. Neighbors can usually be counted on to help when you need them. There is a strong sense of being cared for and supported. The individual is perceived as be-

> There is a destiny that makes us brothers, none goes his way alone. All that we send into the lives of others comes back into our own.
>
> —Edwin Markham

ing a part of a larger community. People who live in these communities for generations become keen observers of and participants in each other's lives. Starratt (1996) described this situation as one in which individuals become absorbed in a communal identity.

An excellent example of this rural strength comes from the life of Marian Wright Edelman, founder and president of the Children's Defense Fund, who grew up in Bennettsville, South Carolina (as quoted in Schorr, 1997):

> I went everywhere with my parents and was under the watchful eye of the congregation and community who were my extended family. They kept me when my parents went out of town, they reported on me and chided me when I strayed from the straight and narrow of community expectations, and they basked in and supported my achievements when I did well. (p. 303)

Of course, rural communities also exhibit some shortcomings. Probably most important is the sense of intrusiveness that comes with small-ness: Everyone knows your business. The balancing act of having a personal, private life and being connected in small communities can be difficult. The sense of privacy that individuals need is rarely found in this setting, which "explains why, for millennia, the dream of rural people was to escape into the city" (Drucker, 1998, p. 3).

Urban and Suburban Communities

Urban communities developed more recently. The industrial revolu-tion of the 19th century drew those who were unhappy with the forced intimacy of rural life and who found the anonym-ity of city life to their liking. Of course, this was not a new phenomenon. The motivation to find free-dom in cities dates back to medieval times and ear-lier, when serfs fled from the country to become free people with privileges of citizenship granted in the cities.

> Few people are capable of expressing with equanimity opinions which differ from the prejudices of their social environment.
>
> —Albert Einstein

Like the serfs, groups of people from many countries left behind oppressive conditions to migrate to the United States. They came to the growing cities where they could preserve and practice their cultures and traditions. In these enclaves, they also found protection from other segments of society that did not understand or accept them.

> Unless justice be done to others, it will not be done to us.
> —Woodrow Wilson

Cities are multifaceted places with a variety of opportunities for income, anonymity, and individuality. This was especially true during much of the 20th century. If you were willing to work and were physically able, jobs were available. People who moved from rural settings felt a new freedom to be themselves because of the diversity and anonymity that existed in the cities. They also viewed the city workplace as compartmentalized from personal life, in contrast to rural settings where work and personal identities were melded into one. Expression of individuality in cities was accepted, whereas it was often difficult to pursue in small, rural communities.

Despite all the benefits individuals could find in cities, and more recently in the many sprawling suburbs that surround them, there was a missing element—the sense of community. Cities presented an enticement that was an alternative to the intrusiveness that rural community people deserted, but this came with a high cost—the loss of the caring, support, and belonging that could be provided by these smaller communities.

There were other problems unique to city life that early dwellers experienced. For example, disease and epidemics were prevalent and shortened

> We won't have a society if we destroy the environment.
> —Margaret Mead

the lives of city dwellers. Cities grew at an alarming rate, and city planning became a major consideration. Most ironic, the influx of people from rural communities as well as immigrant groups reduced the chances of finding and keeping jobs.

In summary, the idyllic picture of the city was as unrealistic as that of the rural setting: It "was attractive precisely because it offered freedom from the compulsory and coercive community. But it was destructive because it did not offer any community of its own" (Drucker, 1998, p. 4).

Without a strong community orientation, a problematic cycle of events can easily be created. The cycle might be described as follows. People move to cities to improve their economic well-being and to shed the intrusiveness of small communities. After an initial period of time, they seek connection through community. As a substitute for the small community, neighborhoods take form and grow. They then go through transitions. Those who were once neighborhood guardians move on. Those left behind become more fearful and isolated from each other. In time, they turn away

> I believe that that community is already in process of dissolution where each man begins to eye his neighbor as a possible enemy, where nonconformity with the accepted creed, political as well as religious, is a mark of disaffection.
> —Judge Learned Hand

from each other and seek any means that are available to provide for their protection and security.

When all is said and done, individuals may feel more secure but at the price of feeling disconnected from neighbors and the larger community. As prosocial bonding opportunities shrink and boundaries become more difficult to define and maintain, individuals seek alternative forms of community. These may come in the form of gangs that provide connections between individuals, especially for those who feel most isolated and alienated. Gangs are a response to the absence of constructive means and ends, whether we are talking about "the gangs of Victorian England, or the gangs that today threaten the very social fabric of the large, American city (and, increasingly, of every large city in the world)" (Drucker, 1998, p. 5).

The evolution of our society from agrarian to urban and suburban has created new challenges. Furthermore, there is no end to the list of possible challenges and obstacles that exist for all of our communities. These include high mobility rates, inequities of earning and housing, fragmentation of values and norms, fear and violence, policies and rules that conflict across government agencies within single communities, rapid advances in technology and communications, an increase in single-parent homes, large corporations that are squeezing neighborhood stores out of business, and a lack of opportunities to gather and celebrate. Just listing these potential stumbling blocks can create a sense among community members that they are insurmountable and promote a fatalistic, "why bother to try to improve the situation?" kind of attitude.

Visualizing the Resilient Community

Our challenge is to create communities that are capable of meeting the needs of their members, many of which appear to be overwhelming or are still not clear to us. How does the notion of community bounded by geographic location fit with the fluidity of today's society? How does the concept of community as we have known it relate to our changing world?

We need to move outside the parameters of our traditional understanding of community if we are going to be able to answer these questions. We need to do this so that new ideas and new behaviors will flourish in ways that promote community resiliency. With the changing scope and size of urbanized centers and the shifting nature of society's major institutions, including the home, the church, and schools, as well as the globalization of economies, redefining and rebuilding communities is vitally important for the health of our own generation and of coming generations. We need to think differently about what a community is and what it looks like: To do this "will require . . . a transformation of our limited understanding of both the individual and of the community" (Starratt, 1996, p. 93).

We can move toward the development of resilient communities, but in most cases not as we have known them in the past. Individuals and groups must discover new ways to work with each other to create sustainable communities.

> Democracy is measured not by its leaders doing extraordinary things, but by its citizens doing ordinary things extraordinarily well.
> —*John Gardner*

Further complicating the situation, especially given our high mobility rate, is electronic communications, which affects our imagery of community. For example, as we search for community, we can easily confuse the simulation of community we see on talk shows with the reality of true community. When we watch our favorite talk show in the comfort of our homes, we may be desperately reaching out for some form of community. Guests may make us feel that we belong as they give us graphic descriptions of their problems. In some cases, there are even protagonists who may plead their alternative versions in front of our surrogates—the studio audience. After the problem has been explored, the audience may even be asked to participate in the discussion, and a few may make statements about the situation while others nod their heads to nonverbally voice their feelings about these assessments. But after the show, everyone goes home. In reality, a temporary community has been established for the half-hour or hour talk show "interaction." This temporary community is a mere facade of a sustainable community. There is no attempt to develop the bonding, boundaries, life skills, care and support, high expectations, or meaningful participation that are needed to respond and build resiliency in a community. There certainly is none of the responsibility that Marian Wright Edelman described about growing up in her community.

> Man must cease attributing his problems to his environment, and learn again to exercise his will—his personal responsibility in the realm of faith and morals.
> —*Albert Schweitzer*

Is this our destiny—to create facades of community? It can be, unless we adapt and change in response to changing realities. If we don't, we may become the vivid nightmare Orwell (1949) described in *1984*, in which he envisioned a highly controlled society where any words in the language that might be conflictual must be eliminated until there are very few "acceptable" words. In *1984*, Big Brother sought to control society with rules, regulations, and standards. The system was repressive rather than responsive. As a result, the community did not thrive and grow.

> I know of no more encouraging fact than the unquestionable ability of man to elevate his life by a conscious endeavor.
> —*Henry David Thoreau*

Resilient communities are those that confront problems in ways that bring individuals and groups together to interact and provide needed support. They are communities in which schools, other governmental agencies, higher education institutions, and voluntary and business organizations join together to plan and develop activities that promote positive, shared experiences and relationships.

Promoting discussions about the strengths and challenges of the community can begin the process of moving it toward resiliency building. What are we trying to change? What are we trying to become? Why is this such an important goal for individuals, groups, and the community? Who should be involved in the discussion? Which allies and key stakeholders need to collaborate in the process?

When people and groups come to understand and accept the challenge to recreate their communities, they will grow and prosper. Key elements of community building include the following:

Knowing one another. Getting to know each other can change community dynamics rapidly and dramatically. An example of this is when a village in Italy found itself confronted with a growing crime problem. All of the business owners and residents were asked to do just one thing: leave their homes 15 minutes early before going to work each day so they could meet and talk with their neighbors. The results of this simple outreach effort were overwhelming. Crime was cut almost in half in just 6 months. People in this Italian village made an effort to get to know their neighbors, which caused them to care about what happened to each other. This was a drastic change—from the sense of fear, isolation, and need to protect themselves from each other, to a willingness to reach out and support each other.

> Perfect valor is to do unwitnessed what we should be capable of doing before all the world.
> —Duc de La Rochefoucauld

Positive relationships. The relationships between community members in the preceding example promoted a healthier community. Neighbors responding to each other in healthy ways can promote positive relationships. Communities that promote relationships are communities that can become healthier. Positive relationships can do much to reduce the sense of isolation and improve the capacity for community building.

> Civilization is a method of living, an attitude of equal respect for all men [and women].
> —Jane Adams

Stability. Change creates instability and unfamiliarity. Schools and communities undergoing change feel tremors, much like tremors are felt during an earthquake. Stability can be created through the development and communication of purposes, expectations, and boundaries. Knowing what the boundaries are helps, as do stable structures, which provide the protection needed while experiencing change.

> I think somehow, we learn who we really are and then live with that decision.
> —Eleanor Roosevelt

Skills and abilities to promote growth and transcend boundaries. To participate effectively as community members, individuals need to learn new skills and improve their abilities. Most important, they need to learn how to cope effectively with the boundaries that proliferate in our complex communities—boundaries between age groups and sociodemographic groups, among voluntary groups, and across different governmental agencies. It is at these boundary points that the system is most vulnerable to change:

> Education has in America's whole history been the major hope for improving the individual and society.
> —Gunnar Myrdal

The very idea of boundaries changes profoundly. Rather than being self-protective walls, boundaries become the place of meeting and exchange. . . . They are the place where new relationships take form, an important place of exchange and growth as one individual chooses to respond to another. As connections proliferate and the system weaves itself into existence, it becomes difficult to interpret boundaries as defenses, or even as markers of where one individual ends. (Wheatley & Kellner-Rogers, 1998a, p. 12)

Connectivity. We need to think about community as an entity, a receptacle that can be used to bring everyone together, rather than as being composed of unique and disparate parts that have little in common. All stakeholders in the community have legitimate roles to play and legitimate ends to serve. As such, participation of representative stakeholders in discussions about ways to strengthen the community is required. There needs to be a balance of voices to uncover ideas that can be explored by all stakeholders. In fact, even one voice can be very powerful, as Rosa Parks reminds us as she moved us to help shape a new community image.

> The only thing necessary for the triumph of evil is for good men to do nothing.
> —Edmund Burke

Engaging collective voices from across the community spectrum can lead to efforts to meet the challenge of promoting community resiliency. Connectivity and participation is the glue that can hold us together to create the foundation for a healthy and resilient community.

Building a Resilient Community: Where Do We Start?

The diversity of life experiences and the untapped talents and skills of all residents are needed to create a resilient community. When voices are heard, positive energy can be created and a sense of belonging and support can be developed throughout the community.

A good starting place is to clarify present attitudes and perceptions about the community. To what extent is it a place that cares, promotes connections, forges relationships, and supports growth? These qualities need to be fostered for a community to be healthy and resilient.

Communities that promote shared values and purposes tend to minimize formal mechanisms of control, focusing more on the development of normative understandings that encourage individuals and groups to come together for the well-being of all. Policies, rules, and structures can provide boundaries and promote stability, but they can also be unresponsive to individual differences and needs. Likewise, policies, rules, and structures can be a big part of the problem, getting in the way of the development of shared values and purposes.

> Take care of yourself.
> Take care of each other.
> Take care of this place.
> —*Margaret Wheatley and Myron Kellner-Rogers*

Radical actions are not always required to improve the health of a community. In fact, changing course a degree or two can, over time, make a powerful difference in moving a community away from dysfunctional behaviors and toward healthy behaviors.

> Act well at the moment, and you have performed a good action to all eternity.
> —*Johann Kaspar Lavater*

Community building does not require that everyone agrees about what needs to be done, but they do have to believe that they matter to each other. If this belief exists and is fostered, anything is possible.

> That action alone is just that does not harm either party to a dispute.
> —*Mohandas Gandhi*

Schools as Starting Places Toward Building Community Resiliency

The often-used saying, "think globally and act locally," is the only realistic way we will begin to move our complex communities, and thus our nation and world, toward the health and resiliency that is so badly needed. Acting locally, taking on the work that needs to be done, piece by piece, is how, over the long haul, the larger community will be positively affected.

> This is still a very wealthy country. The failure is of spirit and insight.
> —*Jerry Brown*

Schools are the "local" focus of this book, not only because we believe that resiliency in schools is so desperately needed for them to achieve their purposes but also because resilient schools have an immediate and direct impact on the improvement of community resiliency. Schools are where community members spend their formative years. They are also likely to be one of the primary places where many community members interact.

Following this local-global logic, the four chapters in Part II are intended to build on each other, beginning with a focus on students (Chapter 3),

> The worst sin towards our fellow creatures is not to hate them, but to be indifferent to them; that's the essence of inhumanity.
> —*George Bernard Shaw*

educators (Chapter 4), the school organization (Chapter 5), and communities (Chapter 6). The same local-global logic can be applied, depending on reader interests, to other governmental agency-total community dynamics (e.g., welfare, higher education, or the justice system).

PART II

RESILIENCY FOR EVERYONE

CHAPTER 3

Student Resiliency

Building a Base for Positive Living

The object of education is to prepare the young to educate themselves throughout their lives.

—Robert Maynard Hutchins

We all know stories about youngsters who overcome extraordinary odds to become productive members of society. Consider these:

* A documentary movie, *Hoop Dreams,* spans the teen years of two African American youths who struggle to overcome the effects of poverty and living in communities replete with antisocial elements. Counterbalancing these negative factors are understanding and supportive home environments, as well as a special talent that they possess—the ability to play basketball extremely well. The movie illustrates the extraordinary difficulties they confront and how, inch by inch, they cope with and overcome many of these difficulties.

* A story is told by Eric Butterworth (related in Canfield & Hansen, 1993) about a professor who asked his students to study 200 young boys from a Baltimore slum and predict what their future lives would be like. The basic conclusion they came to was that these boys would probably not lead very successful lives. A quarter of a century later, another professor asked his students to do a follow-up study and see how things actually turned out for these

young men. Of the 180 now 30-something men that they could find, 176 had defied the odds to live productive lives. Many had even become doctors, lawyers, and businessmen. Wondering how the earlier predictions could be so wrong, the professor asked some of these men to identify the sources of their success. The frequent reply was: "There was a teacher." More specifically, most of them mentioned the *same* teacher. He searched for and found the long-since-retired teacher and asked her what she did to help them become successful. Her straightforward answer was: "It's really very simple, I loved those boys."

* * *

In every child who is born, under no matter what circumstances, and of no matter what parents, the potentiality of the human race is born again.

—James Agee

We tend to think of such stories as exceptions to the rule. In reality, there are many similar stories that we can all recall from our own experiences. What stories come to mind when you think about youth you have known who have overcome significant odds and have succeeded? We are certain that, with very little thought, you can identify many such youngsters.

The intriguing question to explore is, *What is it about them that accounts for their successes, whereas others in similar situations have not succeeded?* In this chapter, we focus on problems that many youth are coping with and why, too often, we seem to be unable to respond to their problems effectively. We then examine how our unconscious problem-solver mind maps contribute to the situation and how we can shift this approach to a more positive and effective approach—resiliency. We discuss various ways to positively affect students' resiliency, focusing on the six resiliency factors introduced in Chapter 1. Last, we explore ways of restructuring our schools as well as our attitudes and beliefs so we can relate more effectively with our students.

The Problems

We often ignore problems faced by youth until they become crises and we are forced to recognize them. A sad example of this pattern of behavior is our response to the rash of killings—of students, parents, teachers, and administrators—committed by young males in a little more than a year, between February 1997 and May 1999, in Alaska, Arkansas, Colorado, Georgia, Kentucky, Michigan, Mississippi, Oregon, Pennsylvania, and Tennessee. These tragedies were sufficiently dramatic and widespread to catch our attention, particularly the most tragic of them: the mass killings at Columbine High School in Littleton, Colorado. It is interesting that they do not really represent an increase in teen homicides—only a change of venue from inner-city to suburban and rural homicides.

Though highly charged, these negative behavioral manifestations of youngsters who are in jeopardy are not isolated events nor are they a new phenomenon. A full decade ago, the Children's Defense Fund's (1990) *Report Card* concluded that on any given day,

- 135,000 children bring a gun to school
- 30 children are wounded by guns
- 10 children die from guns
- 7,742 teens become sexually active
- 623 teenagers get syphilis or gonorrhea
- 2,556 children are born out of wedlock
- 211 children are arrested for drug abuse
- 437 children are arrested for drinking or drunken driving
- 1,629 children are in adult jails
- 1,849 children are abused or neglected
- 3,288 children run away from home
- 2,989 children see their parents divorced
- 6 teenagers commit suicide
- 1,512 teenagers drop out of school

Over the past decade, many efforts have been made to deal with these stark realities, but for the most part, the problems have proved to be rather intractable. In fact, many of the negative trends regarding adolescents were actually diminishing during the 1980s, but during the 1990s, these figures moved back upward. For example, one study noted that

> teenage cigarette smoking is up by as much as 2 percent per year since 1992. Marijuana use has increased for three straight years among 8th, 10th, and 12th grade students. More teens live in poverty now than during the previous decade [and] teenage homicide has increased. (Blum & Rinehart, 1997, p. 5)

Given the energy expended and the minimal positive impact for the effort, most of us shake our heads and wonder, *How could this have happened?* Exercise 3.1 offers a way to take a look at this question.

> There is no greater insight into the future than recognizing when we save our children, we save ourselves.
>
> —Margaret Mead

EXERCISE 3.1. How Could This Have Happened?

This exercise can be used to encourage people (e.g., teachers, parents, or teachers and parents) to share their concerns and suggest why we find ourselves in the difficult situations that exist in many of our communities. In the process, members can get a better picture of the many elements involved and, hopefully, start to develop a commonly held set of beliefs and a clearer set of understandings as a base for taking action.

1. Distribute copies of the Children's Defense Fund findings (Handout 3 in the Resource section). Ask group members to review the findings and discuss which of them seems to be true of communities they know. Ask the group to identify agreements, and record them on a chalkboard or chart paper.

2. Ask the group to review these similarities and themes as they may relate to youngsters in your own community. Which, if any, are observable among the youth of your own community? If information summaries concerning your own community, region, or state are available and are similar to the Children's Defense Fund findings, you might want to distribute them at this point. (Check with the local health department, the police department, the mayor's office, and the central office of the school district for this information.) Lead a discussion and record agreements.

3. Ask the group whether they know of efforts currently under way in the community (by the school district, local government, voluntary groups, or others) that are seeking to respond to these themes. Ask them to share what they know about such efforts. Record group members' thoughts.

4. If there are efforts presently going on, ask the group to explore how effective each is in improving the lives of youths in the community. Where they appear to be successful, explore why this is the case. Where they fall short, explore why this appears to be the situation.

5. Last, ask the group to discuss whether there are ways of addressing the identified shortcomings and, as a way of moving toward positive response, whether they would like to reconvene to talk about next steps.

Changing Our Mind Maps: From Deficits to Potentials

Because we spend so much time and energy talking about problems, we soon come to see everything as just that—problems! Most well-meaning parents, teachers, and administrators are constantly on the watch for problems that youngsters "may" possess (e.g., learning disabilities, short attention spans, antisocial behaviors, and substance abuse).

There certainly are enough problems around for us to worry about. But there is a downside to focusing on problems: We soon come to view things in a myopic and negative fashion, similar to the way many police may see everyone as potential criminals!

This problem-oriented perspective has significant implications for how we deal with youngsters. First, coming from this perspective, we focus our energies on problems children may display. We highlight negative behaviors rather than *all* behaviors, their strengths as well as their shortcomings. Second, coming from this perspective, we tend to generalize from experiences with so-called problem kids we know to any youngsters who appear to have *the potential* to exhibit similar shortcomings. Exercise 3.2 emphasizes the impact of the way we view youngsters.

> When I see the *Ten Most Wanted Lists* . . . I always have this thought: If we'd made them feel wanted earlier, they wouldn't be wanted now.
> —*Eddie Cantor*

> People are always ready to admit a man's ability after he gets there.
> —*Bob Edwards*

EXERCISE 3.2. Strengths or Deficits: What Do You See?

To get the most out of the exercise, *please respond to the instructions in the order they are given*. Provide group members with a page of blank paper, and ask them to do the following:

1. Draw a page-sized, sad-faced stick figure. Label the stick figure "At Risk."
2. Think of a *real* youngster you know who you believe possesses multiple at-risk factors. Risk factors might include environmental realities as well as personal problems, behaviors, and attitudes. As you think of the factors this particular youngster exhibits, write them on the stick figure.
3. Get together with another member of your group. Taking turns, share the risk factors that the two of you have identified regarding both of your youngsters. Listen carefully for commonalities.
4. Ask the group to come together to share risk factors they found to be mentioned most frequently. List them on a chalkboard or on chart paper.
5. Provide a second sheet of blank paper for each group member and ask them to draw another page-length stick figure. Ask them to make this one happy faced, and label it "Resilient." Think about *the same youngster you just identified as exhibiting multiple risk factors*. What does this youngster have going for him or her? These resiliency factors can be environmentally related or emanate from personal behaviors and attitudes. As they come to mind, write them on the resilient stick figure.
6. Share your thoughts about this youngster's resiliency factors with the same partner you talked with in Step 3, and listen carefully for common conclusions as that person shares with you.
7. As with Step 4, ask the group to share the factors that were identified most frequently. Record comments on a chalkboard or on chart paper.
8. Ask group members to reflect on the activity. Did they find it easier to fill in the at-risk stick figure or the resiliency stick figure? Count how many found the at-risk part of the exercise easier to complete. Do the same for the resiliency part of the exercise. Many will probably conclude that it was easier to identify deficits. If this is true for your group, ask members to discuss the implications.

(continued)

EXERCISE 3.2. Continued

9. Ask group members to talk about why it is so important to see their youngsters as possessing resiliency factors as well as risk factors. Could relationships with such youngsters be different if group members focused more on strengths or resiliencies that they possess? Furthermore, would it make a difference in how these youngsters might see themselves? Could it increase the likelihood of these youngsters succeeding in school and in life?

SOURCE: This exercise was adapted from one originally developed by Nan Henderson.

The point of this exercise is clear: *How we perceive others forms the basis of how we relate to them.* When relating with youngsters, we need to be particularly sensitive to this reality because they are just forming their self-images. As Shel Silverstein (1974, p. 27) reminds us, we have a powerful ability to detract or build on their potential for resiliency during their formative years:

> Listen to the MUSTN'TS, child,
> Listen to the DON'TS
> Listen to the SHOULDN'TS
> The IMPOSSIBLES, the WON'TS
> Listen to the NEVER HAVES
> Then listen close to me—
> Anything can happen, child,
> ANYTHING can be
>
> —*Shel Silverstein*

Which is the mind map from which you operate? Is it "the impossibles" mind map or is it the "anything can be" mind map? How about your school's mind map? How about your community's mind map? This is important to think about because, in large part, what we see is what we get! We are not suggesting that problems are irrelevant. If they are real, they must be confronted. But each of us also has extraordinary strengths, capabilities, and potentials.

As parents, educators, and community members, we are guides and role models for today's youth. What we say and do matters. We can add to youngsters' difficulties, we can leave them on their own to cope as best they can, or we can be positive forces in their lives, relating with them in ways that encourage wellness, confidence, and pride in positive achievements. Exercise 3.3 emphasizes the importance of our responses to them.

> If a child lives with approval, he learns to live with himself.
> —*Dorothy Law Nolte*

EXERCISE 3.3. A Judgment Test

1. This activity can be done individually, but it is best done with groups. Distribute copies of the case descriptions that follow (see Handout 4 in the Resource section).

   * Case A. Girl, age 16, orphaned, willed to custody of grandmother by mother who was separated from alcoholic husband, now deceased. Mother rejected the homely child, who had been proven to lie and steal sweets. Swallowed penny to attract attention. Father was fond of the child. Child lived in fantasy as mistress of her father's household for years. The grandmother, who is widowed, cannot manage the girl's four young uncles and aunts in the household. Young uncle drinks, has left home without telling the grandmother his destination. Aunt, emotional over love affair, locks self in room. Grandmother resolved to be stricter with granddaughter because she fears she has failed with her own children. She dresses the granddaughter oddly. She refuses to let her have playmates. Put her in braces to keep her back straight. Did not send her to grade school. Aunt on paternal side of family is crippled, uncle is asthmatic.

   * Case B. Boy, senior in high school, has obtained certificate from physician stating that nervous breakdown makes it necessary for him to leave school for 6 months. Boy is not a good all-around student; has no friends; teachers find him to be a problem, developed speech late; has had poor adjustment to school; and father is ashamed of son's lack of athletic ability. Boy has odd mannerisms; makes up his own religion, chants hymns to himself—parents regard him as "different."

   * Case C. Boy, age 6, head large at birth. Thought to have had brain fever (meningitis). Three siblings died before his birth. Mother does not agree with relatives and neighbors that the child is probably abnormal. Child is sent to school and is diagnosed as mentally ill by the teacher. Mother is angry—withdraws child from school, saying she will teach him herself.

2. After reading the three cases, group members should discuss their predictions:
   • How will each of these young people function as they grow up?
   • Will they be gifted, average-normal, psychotic, neurotic, delinquent, or mentally deficient?
   • Will they excel or will they lead very difficult lives? Ask members why they have come to these conclusions.

3. Last, look at the additional information about these cases that is provided in Handout 5 in the Resource section and respond to the question posed there.

Emmy Werner and Ruth Smith's (1992) classic study of at-risk youth on the Hawaiian Island of Kauai is an extraordinary longitudinal study that documents the human capacity to "overcome the odds." In summary,

1. Their longitudinal study includes all of the survivors of the 837 individuals born on Kauai in 1955, from their prenatal period and, currently, into their forties.

2. About two thirds grew up with sufficient support to function as effective youngsters and as adults.

3. The other one third were identified as "high risk" because they had multiple risk factors in their lives, including prenatal stress, chronic poverty, and family situations marked by parents with some mix of low education, alcoholism, and mental disturbance.

4. About a third of these high-risk children seemed invulnerable to risk factors. They led healthy lives as adolescents and developed into normal young adults by the end of their teen years. Their human drive to survive and succeed apparently helped them overcome the worst adversities that high-risk individuals confront.

5. The rest of the high-risk children (about two thirds) did develop problems by the age of 10 (e.g., delinquency and mental health problems). However, the majority of the individuals in this group were doing well by the time they reached their thirties. This is one of the most important findings of the study. That is, although many of those who were identified as likely to exhibit high-risk behavior did indeed do so, *it was not a one-way street. Most found their way back by their early adult years.*

6. Only a small number of the original high-risk group (about one sixth of them) continued to exhibit problems as adults.

What accounts for the fact that the majority of those who exhibited risk behaviors during their younger years turned out to be more resilient than was anticipated? A number of conclusions were drawn by Werner and Smith (1992), the most important of which were these:

- Leaving their homes of origin gave many a new lease on life.
- Some joined the military and thrived within the required behavioral boundaries, gained new skills, were encouraged to achieve, and participated in experiences that were meaningful to them.
- Many married, became parents, and joined church groups.
- Someone along the way reached out with the message that "you matter" and "it doesn't matter what you have done in the past."
- They developed competencies that were valued by others.

- Sources of support were available to them—most often from neighbors, teachers, and youth leaders. Such support individuals or groups became, in effect, their extended families. The care and support provided appear to be the most important elements that helped these high-risk participants make it through their hardest times.

The findings of Werner and Smith's (1992) ongoing Kauai study, and those of similar longitudinal studies (e.g., Anthony & Cohler, 1987; Elder, Liker, & Cross, 1984; Farrington, 1989; Higgins, 1985; Rutter, 1989) are important guides for present purposes. What these studies tell us is what we should already know through our own life's experiences and through the lives of others that have come back from extremely deficit situations—*most people are amazingly resilient.*

> I have never taught an "at-risk" student in my life.
> —Herbert Kohl

The title of Werner and Smith's (1992) book, *Overcoming the Odds,* though not intended, implies that individuals who exhibit resiliency are on their own when trying to overcome negative environments. On the contrary, with positive support from the environment—schools, families, and communities—we can *change the odds.* We need to do this so that more youngsters avoid engaging in risky behaviors. For those who are already exhibiting risk behavior, we need to help them work through their difficulties easier, faster, and with fewer negative repercussions.

What happens when schools are unable or unwilling to help troubled youngsters? Some who drop out or are pushed out of school may find sufficient support in the alternative schools that have been developed in many school districts. These alternative schools can be settings where such youngsters gain the balance they need to get back on track, succeed academically, and pursue meaningful and positive lives.

Others may find their way back from risk behavior by becoming involved in community-based organizations. McLaughlin, Irby, and Langman (1994) provide convincing evidence that "sanctuaries," varying from local storefront organizations to nationally known organizations, such as the YMCA, can encourage youngsters to become engaged in positive, proactive activities (e.g., theater or athletics). These organizations provide the support, security, caring relationships, and opportunities for achievement that can make the difference between a life fraught with problems and a life that is positive and productive.

Many youngsters who attend alternative schools or participate in community-based organizations, or both, manage to do well and become more resilient. Why don't these same youngsters succeed in regular public schools? Many of them do much better in other settings, so it can't just be the students' fault. We need to focus on the school environment. We need to change schools in ways that can help youngsters succeed as students and as people. This calls for conscious efforts on the schools' part to develop youngsters' resiliency.

> Likely as not, the child you can do the least with will do the most to make you proud.
> —Mignon McLaughlin

Student Resiliency:
The Community and
School's Responsibilities

Chapter 1 presented a list of internal and environmental protective factors (Table 1.1). The extent to which these factors exist in our lives directly affects our ability to exhibit resiliency, whether as children, adolescents, or adults. How can we help youngsters develop resiliency profiles that are replete with these factors? Changing the way we respond to students' resiliency needs begins with an honest assessment of how we interact with students right now. Exercise 3.4 can provide an initial assessment of your school's current situation.

EXERCISE 3.4. Are We Supporting Youngsters' Protective Factors?

1. Distribute copies of Table 1.1 (Handout 2 in the Resource section). Ask group members to assess the extent to which "typical" youngsters in your school possess them. Which are most present? Which are least present?
2. How present are these factors among youngsters who seem to be at risk?
3. Are there differences between the extent to which (so-called) typical and at-risk youngsters possess protective factors? If so, discuss whether the school is doing anything that may be contributing to these differences.
4. Discuss what the school may need to do, or do more effectively, to help *all* youngsters acquire these resiliency factors.

Another way of proceeding with this assessment might be to use the approach developed by the Search Institute, a nonprofit organization based in Minneapolis, Minnesota. The Search Institute has surveyed parents and youngsters in communities across the country to identify what it calls *developmental assets*, which are similar in nature to the internal and environmental protective factors but are more specifically focused on the needs of young people (Benson, 1997; Benson, Galbraith, & Espeland, 1995). The extent to which external assets (e.g., parent support, communication, involvement, positive school climate, and involvement in school extracurricular activities) and internal assets (e.g., achievement motivation, homework, helping others, assertiveness skills, and self-esteem) exist directly affects youngsters' levels of resiliency. The Search Institute has correlated such behavioral indicators as extent of alcohol use, early sexual experience, and school success with the number of assets that are present in the environment as well as within the individual. The Search Institute believes that the

> This is our village
> These are our children
> Love them
> Teach them
> Guide them
> —*Anonymous, Battle Creek, Michigan billboard (2/15/98)*

more assets that are in existence, the less risk-related behavior will be evidenced and the more school success will be seen.

Strategies That Promote Student Resiliency

In all likelihood, your school has probably already developed many responses to student resiliency needs. However, unless your approach is *comprehensive and focuses on basic resiliency factors rather than on the symptoms that happen to be displayed,* these efforts may lead to meager results. Figure 3.1 illustrates this clearly.

Our hope is that students will possess the positive characteristics noted in the upper left-hand corner of Figure 3.1. However, the sad reality is that many of our students are burdened by the barriers to learning identified on the wall and the box of problems being dragged along.

With the best of intentions, we fund programs for certain classifications of students (e.g., at-risk and those needing compensatory education) and

Figure 3.1. Learning Barriers and Responses

provide special programs (e.g., substance abuse and remedial reading) to try to meet their specific needs. What we should be doing is taking a holistic approach, placing it in a larger societal perspective, and recognizing that the specific manifestations we are observing are often symptoms of deeper problems. Students with low resiliency will always find creative ways of acting out, including exhibiting learning problems or other difficult behaviors, such as low school attendance, substance abuse, teen pregnancies, gang activities, and violence. Certainly, we need to respond to these symptomatic realities, but we also need to address the deeper problems that they represent. We need to get to the taproot, *the absence or paucity of factors that promote resiliency.* This is the only way we will ever reduce the potential for the dysfunctional behaviors that are associated with low resiliency.

A number of suggestions follow for improving youngsters' resiliency at your school. *We encourage you to engage educators and parents in discussions that can modify and improve on the six resiliency factors in ways that are appropriate to your situation and to add other suggestions that might be worth implementing.*

Increase Prosocial Bonding

If we do not provide opportunities for prosocial bonding, youngsters will find other ways to satisfy their bonding needs. That is the way of human nature. Gangs exist because they fill a bonding void for many youngsters. Gang membership may be viewed as antisocial bonding, but it clearly fills a bonding need. We need to provide as many prosocial bonding opportunities as we can, to engage youngsters effectively, especially if we hope to make gang membership less desirable.

> The key to effective prevention efforts is to reinforce within every arena, the natural social bonds between young and old, between siblings, between friends that give meaning to one's life and a . . . reason for commitment and caring.
> —Emmy Werner

Strategies for Increasing Prosocial Bonding

- Promote good relationships with supportive adults as well as positive peer bonding opportunities within the school.
- Provide a variety of extracurricular activities before, during, and after school that might appeal to different interests. The possibilities are rich and varied, including athletics, theater and the arts, service clubs, and academic enrichment opportunities.

- Diversify teaching approaches by encompassing multiple intelligences to account for different ways of learning. Besides promoting academic success, diversification of teaching approaches can encourage students to become more involved with classroom and school dynamics.

- Encourage family involvement to promote a sense of shared purposes between parents, children, and the school. This is easier to accomplish at the elementary school level, but although more difficult, it is just as important to encourage parental involvement at the middle and high school levels. To do so, we need to identify relevant and real roles for parent involvement (e.g., as members of site-based management teams, teacher assistants, and mentors) and develop approaches that include them as part of their children's' learning teams. We need to reach out and contact parents much more regularly and more often. We need to put more emphasis on sharing good news with them and less emphasis on delivering bad news.

- Create smaller teacher-student groupings within schools to counteract the negative effects of large schools. Subunits such as "families" and "houses" can provide a sense of belonging as well as more opportunities for bonding.

Record other strategies that might work to increase prosocial bonding for students:

- _____
  _____
- _____
  _____
- _____
  _____

Set Clear and Consistent Boundaries

Freedom, creativity, and growth are nurtured by setting realistic and appropriate boundaries that can give youngsters a sense of security and safety. Boundaries are especially important for troubled youth, who often view schools as their only sanctuaries from the chaos that otherwise dominates their lives. But a school can only provide such a sanctuary if attention is given to setting boundaries that make it a safe and secure setting for students.

> Our aim is to discipline for activity, for work, for good; not for immobility, not for passivity, not for obedience.
>
> —Maria Montessori

Strategies for Promoting Clear
and Consistent Boundaries

- Develop boundary-related consequences that are clearly stated and appropriate.

- Involve students in the development of boundaries that are meaningful to them.

- Make caring and support the basis for the development of boundaries instead of viewing boundaries as discipline or punishment of misbehavior. This attitude is best reflected if boundary-related language is stated positively and focuses on positive academic and social behaviors. For example, "students have the right to be drug free, to be respected, and to learn in conducive environmental conditions."

- Disseminate clear policies regarding boundaries to all involved— parents and educators as well as students—and actively seek their feedback and suggestions for improvements.

Record other strategies that might help promote clear and consistent boundaries for students:

- _____
  _____

- _____
  _____

- _____
  _____

Teach Life Skills

Schools have choices. They can be baby-sitting establishments that do little more than focus on containment, or they can try to provide education for the basics—reading, writing, and arithmetic—or they can extend their efforts to include helping students develop life skills. Recently, there has been a growing recognition that youth are more likely to exhibit resiliency if they learn skills that equip them to cope effectively with the challenges of life. In fact, formal programs, such as *Emotional Intelligence,* which focuses on helping students make their emotions work for them (Goleman, 1995), and *Character Counts,* which focuses on universal principles of ethics and character, such as respect and responsibility (Lickona, 1991), have been developed to help guide schools in their efforts to bolster students' life skills. As we increase our consensus about what children need to learn and know beyond the academic basics so they can cope well as adults, we should see expanding efforts to provide opportunities for life skill development in schools.

Too often, we give children answers to remember rather than problems to solve.
—Roger Lewin

Strategies for Fostering Life Skills

- Emphasize cooperative learning approaches. Students can develop communications, conflict management, and assertiveness skills that will help them get along with others. They can also learn how to set meaningful goals and make better decisions through cooperative learning.

- Enrich the curriculum so that it focuses on such life skills as assertiveness, refusal skills, conflict resolution, decision making, problem solving, and stress management. This curriculum should be woven throughout the instructional program, but it can also be an integral part of specific courses, such as civics or health.

- Integrate life skills into daily school activities—on the playground, in the lunchroom, and at extracurricular activities, as well as in the regular academic program.

Record other strategies that might increase life skills for students:

- _____
  _____
- _____
  _____
- _____
  _____

Provide Caring and Support

Caring and support are key foundations of resiliency. If we are not cared for, we are likely to feel alienated and alone. Too many youngsters feel this way, especially those who are latchkey children or who live in sterile or alienating homes and communities. Schools often add to their problems if they are excessively large or when high teacher-student ratios make it difficult to provide the focused attention that youngsters require. However, even under these debilitating conditions, caring and support can be provided.

> To have another individual express belief in you as a worthy human being in spite of your acne, awkwardness, and inexperience can be overwhelming.
> —*James J. Fenwick*

Strategies for Enhancing Caring and Support

- Know students by name.
- Identify and focus on individual students' needs and strengths.
- Be empathetic to students' school, home, and community situations.
- Encourage students to participate in learning situations.

- Provide opportunities for team or cooperative learning.
- Recognize and reward positive behaviors by, for example, showing appreciation for doing good class work.
- Encourage youngsters to share their concerns, and provide positive feedback when they try to overcome them.
- Provide concentrated time blocks within the day and throughout the year for teachers and students to connect meaningfully.
- Schedule teacher assignments so they stay with their students, preferably for several years, as students progress from grade to grade.

Record other strategies that might work to enhance care and support for students:

- _____
  _____
- _____
  _____
- _____
  _____

Set and Communicate High Expectations

The message that needs to be sent is "You can do it, and I will support you in any way possible to help you do it!" Too often, however, schools focus on control and orderliness and send the message, "Be quiet, behave well, do the minimum amount of academic work that is required, and you will get along and make it through school!" Many youngsters receive these same kind of disincentive-oriented messages at home and in their community. The human spirit seeks opportunities for challenge, creativity, and growth. School should be a place where this spirit is encouraged, not dampened!

> My idea of education is to unsettle the minds of the young and inflame their intellects.
>
> —Robert Maynard Hutchins

Strategies to Strengthen High Expectations

- Develop incentive programs that promote *every* student's potential to succeed. Create specific and realistic expectations for each student, and provide challenges that are both feasible and relevant. If students are allowed to participate in setting these expectations, they will be more motivated to accomplish them. The emphasis should be on competition with self rather than with others. This can be promoted by practicing and modeling cooperative learning principles and approaches.

- Make it clear that you believe your students can achieve and that you support them in their efforts to do so. A well-known example of this approach is Jaime Escalante's successful efforts to encourage his lower-socioeconomic students to excel in math, particularly calculus, as described in the movie, *Stand and Deliver*. He believed that his students were capable of higher-order thinking, and he challenged them to do so. They responded and accomplished things well beyond what many believed they were capable of accomplishing!

- Encourage students to develop their interests and talents. Each of us has particular talents and skills that, if promoted, can build self-confidence as well as belief in our ability to achieve.

- Place responsibility for learning on students. Encourage them to set their own goals, search out appropriate learning content and activities, solve problems, and think critically so they can develop their own expectations for high achievement.

- Match teaching strategies with each student's learning style. For example, apply Gardner's (1983) schema of multiple intelligences, and vary instructional approaches to challenge students in ways that maximize their potentials to excel.

- Encourage students to support each other's successes in school and in life.

Record other strategies that might strengthen high expectations for students:

- _____
  _____
- _____
  _____
- _____
  _____

Provide Opportunities for Meaningful Participation

Students need to be viewed as participants in a learning community, not as the school's "customers." We get trapped in the student-as-customer mentality when we view educators as permanent residents and students as temporary participants. Certainly, students play different roles than educators, but they have their own legitimate and important stakes in the life of the school beyond the classroom level. Thought of in this way, schools can be laboratories for social development. They are the places where stu-

> If [schools] are able to teach young people to have a critical mind and a socially oriented attitude, they will have done all that is necessary. Students will then become equipped with those qualities which are prerequisite for citizens living in a healthy democratic society.
> —*Albert Einstein*

dents spend most of their waking hours for much of their young lives. They are the places where students, as well as educators, do their work. If we recognize this reality and see schools as laboratories for life skills development, we will seek ways of meaningfully engaging students.

Strategies for Improving Meaningful Participation

- Promote student participation in school governance. Examples of areas for meaningful student participation include discipline and extracurricular committees. Not-so-obvious examples include site-based committees as well as curriculum committees. A review of policy-making needs and governance procedures and actions can likely lead to identification of numerous other possibilities.
- Develop service learning initiatives, which have the added potential of enhancing partnerships between the school and the community.
- Provide opportunities to participate in communication initiatives, such as school newspapers and school-based radio and television stations that can be organized and operated by students.

Record other strategies that might improve meaningful participation of students:

- _____
  _____
- _____
  _____
- _____
  _____

In the real world, it is impossible to categorize these six resiliency factors tightly or to focus on them discretely. Rather, they cross over and affect each other directly and deeply. Ignoring any of them or placing too much emphasis on any single element can result in minimal positive impact. Resilient youngsters don't just happen—most need help in developing their resiliency. As your school initiates changes that are supportive of improving youngsters' resiliency levels in specific areas, give thought to how these changes are likely to affect other resiliency areas.

Encourage Teachers to Work With Students and Parents to Create Resiliency-Building Contracts

The resiliency contract that follows is an example of how to put into practice what we are encouraging. Developing a contract between students, parents, and teachers can help promote a balanced, across-the-board approach to resiliency. It brings the three interested parties together to design

TABLE 3.1   Improving Student Resiliency: A Contract

Resiliency Element	Strengths	Areas for Improvement
Prosocial bonding		
Clear and consistent boundaries		
Life skills		
Caring and support		
High expectations		
Meaningful participation		

Signed by: _____ Student   Date: _____

_____ Parent

_____ Teacher

an educational plan that fits each specific student's resiliency-building needs. Preferably, this should be done at the outset of the school year, as a contract that is tailor-made to fit the student's priority resiliency needs. The process works as follows:

> The habits we form from childhood make no small difference, but rather they make all the difference.
>
> —Aristotle

- The teacher leads the student and parent(s) through a brief discussion of the six resiliency factors.

- Together they assess the student's current situation regarding each of the factors, focusing on both strengths and areas in need of improvement.

- They agree on goals and activities to pursue that are appropriate for each resiliency factor.

- The teacher helps the student and parent(s) understand the importance of all three contract signers' playing their appropriate roles in pursuing the goals and activities that will promote the student's resiliency, monitoring progress that is being made, making modifications that may be needed, and celebrating successes as they occur.

Table 3.1 is a prototype of such a contract (see Handout 6 in the Resource section for a copy of the contract). Readers are encouraged to modify the categories in ways that may best meet their own particular needs. Taking the situation of each youngster into account and proceeding accordingly, we believe that even very young children have the ability to play a part in resiliency contract building.

This chapter has centered on the need to prioritize students' resiliency development needs and has provided a variety of strategies to help accomplish this important goal. There is growing evidence that schools can change and, in the process, positively support the resiliency of youngsters. Examples can be found in Henderson and Milstein (1996), who document the process and impact of resiliency-building efforts in the Albuquerque Public Schools, and in Krovetz (1999), who documents resiliency strategies that are being applied in seven elementary and secondary schools in the area around San Jose, California.

However, this goal is not likely to be attained if we limit our efforts to student resiliency. Youth will not be encouraged to exhibit resiliency unless the adults in their lives act as positive resiliency role models. In Chapter 4, we turn our attention to the importance of promoting educator resiliency and explore ways to go about pursuing this important activity.

CHAPTER 4

Educator Resiliency
Nurturing the Nurturers

A teacher affects eternity; no one can tell where his influence stops.

—Henry Adams

Fostering educator resiliency should be a priority if we expect to have a positive impact on students and communities. Educators who are not resilient will probably be dissatisfied and frustrated. More important, they will be poor role models for their students. In fact, they are likely to be roadblocks rather than pathways for the development of students' resiliency.

This chapter is devoted to helping educators develop and exhibit characteristics of career resiliency so they can remain vital and contribute positively to the goals of their schools. We begin by examining why there seems to be a serious shortage of resilient educators. Then we present information about a widespread phenomena that may contribute to the problem—educator plateauing. Last, we explore strategies that can be employed to change the situation in ways that enable more educators to be more resilient.

Why There Is a Shortage of Resilient Educators

Educators, like most any other professional group, can be divided into three subsets of practitioners: (a) those who somehow find ways of remaining resilient throughout their careers, (b) those who go through periods of low resiliency but manage to find ways of bouncing back, and (c) those who seem to be unable to maintain their enthusiasm or to even function at minimally effective levels.

> Mere survival is an affliction. What is of interest is life, and the direction of that life.
> —Guy Fregault

The first group includes those who always seem to exhibit resiliency—the countless number of educators who find ways to be enthusiastic about their professional activities, year in and year out. They grow and adapt by employing a variety of strategies, including shifting roles, changing their job content and how they deliver it, seeking professional development opportunities, and taking on new challenges. They seem to have an intuitive sense of the importance of growing and becoming all they are capable of becoming. In short, they work at remaining resilient.

> But if a man happens to find himself . . . he has a mansion which he can inhabit with dignity all the days of his life.
> —James Michener

The second group is composed of educators who have exhibited low resiliency at one time or another but somehow have managed to find their way back to commitment, enthusiasm, and involvement. Sometimes, such transformations come through personal decision making, as in the case of a highly senior teacher who served on seemingly endless committees and watched reform efforts come and go. After many years, she began to complain about being worn out and used up. However, after much reflection and feelings of discomfort, she concluded that her students were too important to abandon. She could not quit on them, she refocused, made numerous home visits, and challenged her students to succeed. Through these efforts, she became known, once again, as a caring educator who was able to help many youngsters who otherwise might have dropped out of school.

> There are only two lasting bequests we can hope to give our children. One of these is roots; the other, wings.
> —Hodding Carter

Sometimes, finding the way back may require a little boost from others, such as when a 20-year veteran teacher who seemed to be coasting toward retirement was challenged by his principal to improve his classroom performance. The teacher confided that he had an idea for a curriculum unit that he had long wanted to develop but felt constrained because it would require about $1,000 for materials and equipment. The principal responded by calling the superintendent and obtaining the necessary resources. After overcoming his initial disbelief that someone would actually listen to him and, further, respond positively, the teacher became highly enthusiastic and proceeded to develop a good curriculum unit. In the process, he rekindled an excitement for teaching and spent his final 5 teaching years sharing his enthusiasm and expertise with other teachers. Most important, he started to have a more positive impact on students. These are impressive results. For a minimal financial investment of $1,000, a teacher was reenergized. The district's expenditure of approximately $200,000 for the last 5 years of his teaching was used for good purposes. The hundreds of students who passed through his classroom during these 5 years were affected positively rather than negatively.

Last, there is the third group—educators who appear to be stuck and who feel miserable. It may sound like a line from a western song, but we recently heard one downtrodden teacher comment about his work life in the following manner: "I mind my own business. Every day, I go from my truck to my classroom and back to my truck." We all know of educators—administrators, teachers, and others, who seem to "go between their truck and their classroom," avoiding anything that might be viewed as a challenge or a risk and counting the days until the end of the week, counting

> Things are not as bad as they seem. They are worse.
>
> —Bill Press

> And nothing to look backward to with pride,
> And nothing to look forward to with hope.
>
> —Robert Frost

the weeks until vacation time, and counting the years until retirement. Besides being unhappy individuals, such educators are hardly likely to be good role models for students.

We need to promote a healthy, self-confident, effective workforce if we expect educators to be willing and able to support the resiliency needs of students. Two decades of continuous criticism and ceaseless reform efforts have left the education workforce, which is still highly senior in composition, feeling embattled and under siege. It is clearly time to focus on the resiliency of educators, both for their own well-being and for the well-being of their students.

Just as students need resiliency to develop and thrive at school and in life, educators need career resiliency to develop and thrive as professionals and as people. Career resiliency characteristics include "teamwork, effective communication, adaptability to change, positive and flexible attitudes, continuous learning, self-confidence, willingness to take risks, and a commitment to personal excellence" (Brown, 1996, p. 1). To start the discussion about educator resiliency in your school, Exercise 4.1 encourages members of your group to engage in storytelling about educators who have struggled to remain resilient.

Plateauing

Plateauing is a phenomenon that can directly affect educator resiliency. But before reading about plateauing, it is important that you first respond to the questionnaire presented in Table 4.1. *Respond, as you believe things actually are for you and not as you might want them to be.* To obtain accurate results, be sure to follow the instructions closely as you complete the ques-

---

EXERCISE 4.1. Tell Your Stories

There are probably many interesting educators who have spent some or all of their professional careers at your school. Their stories can provide important lessons regarding what needs to be done by and for educators at the school today. The exercise is most meaningful, both in richness of discussion and potential for change and improvement, if it is shared by the school staff as a group.

1. Think about educators who were on staff at your school at an earlier time and appeared to make it through one or more career crises. That is, they began to lose energy for the job, or they went into a slump, but somehow regained their enthusiasm and focus.
2. Share your stories. Ask group members to share what seemed to cause these crises, and, as important, what do they think these educators did to respond effectively to their crises? Were there noticeable changes or improvements in their work?
3. What about other educators who were on the school's staff and went through career crises but were unable or unwilling to regain their enthusiasm? What can be learned from these individuals' stories? Were there noticeable changes or losses in their work effectiveness?
4. What important lessons can be drawn from the discussion by the group?

---

tionnaire and transfer your results to the scoring sheet (Table 4.2; these are Handouts 7 and 8 in the Resource section).

TABLE 4.1   Educator Plateauing Survey

Select the response that best completes each item, using a scale from 1 to 5, with 1 indicating *strongly agree*, 2 indicating *agree*, 3 indicating *undecided*, 4 indicating *disagree*, and 5 indicating *strongly disagree.*

1. ___ The realities of my job come close to matching my initial expectations.
2. ___ I have high professional regard for those in leadership positions in my organization's structure.
3. ___ I feel trapped because I am unable to advance in my organization.
4. ___ My work is satisfying to me.
5. ___ I feel burdened with the many things I am responsible for in my life.
6. ___ I am bored in my current job.
7. ___ I usually start a new day with a sense of enthusiasm.
8. ___ To the extent that I am interested, I have opportunities to advance in my organization.
9. ___ Work is the most important thing in my life.
10. ___ My job is full of repetitive tasks.

TABLE 4.1   Continued

11. ___ I feel like I have been passed over when advancement opportunities have occurred in my organization.
12. ___ I can usually find time to engage in leisure activities that I enjoy.
13. ___ I have little interest in advancing within my organization's structure.
14. ___ My life is too predictable.
15. ___ I participate in challenging and meaningful activities in my job.
16. ___ I believe I can achieve my career goals within my organization's structure.
17. ___ I have been in my job too long.
18. ___ I find myself being impatient too often with family and friends.
19. ___ I wish I had more opportunities to advance in my organization so I could do more meaningful work.
20. ___ I know my job too well.
21. ___ I rarely think of my life as boring.
22. ___ Although I would like to advance in my organization, given my abilities, my present position is the highest I can realistically attain in my organization.
23. ___ My job affords me little opportunity to learn new things.
24. ___ I am energized by the challenges and opportunities in my job.
25. ___ I consider myself a risk taker in my approach to life.
26. ___ Advancing further in my organization's structure would require that I give up many of the things I really like about my current position.
27. ___ I feel I perform successfully in my current job.
28. ___ My family and friends get irritated with me for being more involved with work than I am with other aspects of my life.
29. ___ My life is turning out as well as I hoped it would.
30. ___ I relate career success to promotion within my organization's structure.

As a reminder, after responding to all items on the survey, please be sure you have

1. Put your responses in the correct places
2. Reversed the scores for those items that are asterisked on the scoring form (i.e., a score of 1 becomes a 5, a 2 becomes a 4, a 3 remains a 3, a 4 becomes a 2, and a 5 becomes a 1)
3. Divided each of the subscale scores by 10
4. Divided your total score by 30

TABLE 4.2   Educator Plateauing Survey Scoring Sheet

The numbers in categories A, B, and C correspond to the 30 statements in the Plateauing Survey. Transfer your responses to the blanks provided. *Note:* Those numbers that are followed by an asterisk (*) are reverse-scoring items. For these items, a score of 1 should be entered as 5, 2 becomes 4, 3 remains 3, 4 becomes 2, and 5 becomes 1. *Be sure to reverse these items as noted.*

Category A	*Category B*	*Category C*
1. _____	2. _____	5.* _____
4. _____	3.* _____	7. _____
6.* _____	8. _____	9.* _____
10.* _____	11.* _____	12. _____
15. _____	13. _____	14.* _____
17.* _____	16. _____	18.* _____
20.* _____	19.* _____	21. _____
23.* _____	22.* _____	25. _____
24. _____	26. _____	28.* _____
27. _____	30.* _____	29. _____

Category Totals (add each column):   *Plateau Area:*

A = _____ Divide by 10 = _____ Content (work has become routine)
B = _____ Divide by 10 = _____ Structure (organization doesn't offer opportunity for growth or promotion)
C = _____ Divide by 10 = _____ Life (life is too predictable or not fulfilling)
Total = ___ Divide by 30 = _____ Overall plateauing

The higher the score in each category and overall, the higher the level of plateauing. This survey can be used to assess the need for resiliency building in any of the three plateauing categories or regarding overall plateauing.

Copyright © 1993 by Mike Milstein.

Before analyzing the meaning of your scores, here is some important background information about plateauing (a good basic source is Bardwick's, 1986, *The Plateauing Trap*):

1. Plateauing is a normal human experience. Throughout life, we vary between periods of high energy, or change and transformation spurts, and periods of calm and quiet, or plateauing. In the normal course of events, plateauing is that period when we reflect, recharge, and prepare for the next transformation or time of change.

2. Plateauing becomes problematic when we feel stuck in a place and have little reason to expect any change or improvement. When we find ourselves experiencing this kind of plateauing, we may feel dissatisfied and concerned about our situation, but we rarely consciously and fully recognize what is happening as we slowly lose enthusiasm, feel less energized, and a sense of hopelessness sets in. Worst of all, because we are probably embarrassed about it, we are not likely to discuss our unease openly with others. In fact, we may come to the conclusion that we are the only ones experiencing these feelings. It requires only a small jump in logic to conclude that there is probably something wrong with us.

3. As the survey scoring sheet indicates, there are three types of plateauing: content, structure, and life.

Content

This type of plateauing has to do with your specific work role. After about 3 to 5 years in a job, most of us have learned how to meet basic role expectations. That is, we become so-called experts. Being experts, we may be less likely to continue to learn, grow, and seek new challenges. It is likely that our jobs will start to feel routine and boring.

After enough time and experience, the learning curve inevitably goes down in any job. Unless we consciously and actively explore ways of responding to this reality, we, and those we work with, can suffer negative consequences—loss of enthusiasm, reduced productivity, and less energy put into cooperative efforts and caring relationships.

Responses to this natural phenomenon vary from educator to educator. Those who do not fully comprehend what is happening to them or believe there is no way out of the situation will feel frustrated, trapped in their roles, and slowly begin to disengage. Others who recognize that they are experiencing manifestations of plateauing and are proactive may try to modify how they conduct their established roles so they will feel more motivated about work. Some may even try out new roles, such as changing schools, changing grade levels, moving into central office positions, or switching from teaching to administration.

Structure

This type of plateauing has to do with the sense of not being appropriately rewarded for your positive contributions or not being able to grow or advance in your organization. This perception can be alleviated for teachers if opportunities exist to take on new roles, such as counselors, diagnosticians, or administrators. Administrators at school sites can be offered the challenge to take on leadership roles at the central office.

Opportunities can also be provided for professional growth and recognition without having to change roles. For example, many teachers who have learned the basic requirements of their roles still desire to extend their abilities through professional development opportunities. Others may seek recognition for their special abilities by taking on new challenges, such as becoming demonstration teachers or acting as mentors for new teachers.

Structural plateauing is experienced differently by different individuals, depending on their perceptions and interests. For example, a teacher who is still highly enthusiastic about teaching will probably have little interest in being promoted out of the classroom but will likely be interested in professional development opportunities that can be applied to classroom activities. However, a teacher who has lost enthusiasm for teaching—is content plateaued and is conscious of the negative effects of the situation—is more likely to be attracted by opportunities to change job roles.

Life

> The ultimate value of life depends upon awareness and the power of contemplation rather than upon mere survival.
>
> —Aristotle

This type of plateauing has to do with the quality of life outside the workplace, especially the quality of relationships with family, relatives, and friends. It also has to do with enthusiasm and motivation for avocations, service, and other normal aspects of life. It is about life's quality, not quantity, about life's intensity and intrinsic worth, not material wealth.

Life plateauing affects different educators differently. Some of those who experience work-related plateauing may find that it can spill over and leave little enthusiasm or energy for high-quality engagement within their nonwork lives. For such educators, all of life becomes a struggle. For others who are plateaued at work, active engagement with life can be viewed as an effective way of minimizing the most negative effects of their work situations. However, although such educators may be better off personally, their professional engagement at work probably will not improve. Last, for those who are not plateaued at work, there may, ironically, be a significant cost in the form of life plateauing. Being highly engaged with work, they may have little energy left to put into nonwork situations. Spouses, children, and friends often adjust by keeping some distance, partly to honor these educators' desires to focus on work-related activities and partly out of self-defense.

Nobody wants to be put into a position where they seem to be tolerated or ignored. With the background information just provided and with your plateauing instrument completed, you can now assess your plateauing level in Exercise 4.2. This exercise can be done individually or can be discussed by the group as a stimulus for support and as encouragement for change (Instrument and Score sheet: Handouts 7 and 8).

> The important thing is not to stop questioning.
>
> —Albert Einstein

Plateauing, as noted, is quite normal. We all experience it. For the main part, it is healthy, a time of reflection, and should not be viewed as a problem or an embarrassment. It can, however, become a problem if and

---

EXERCISE 4.2. How Plateaued Are You?

1. The *average* score for educators taking the instrument is 2.6. This means that a score *above* 2.6 is higher in plateauing and a score *below* 2.6 is lower in plateauing than the average respondent's. The further away your score is, above or below 2.6, the higher or lower your level of plateauing. An examination of your mean scores for each of the three subscales and for the overall questionnaire can provide a picture of your content, structure, and life plateauing, as well as your overall level of plateauing.
2. Check your overall score for a gross indicator of plateauing, but also check the three subscale scores. Which is highest? Which is lowest? Why do you think this is the case?
3. You may want to measure your scores against your own expectations for growth and development, as well as against results of the average respondent. In addition, whether your scores are lower or higher than the 2.6 indicator, there are probably some differences across the three scales, as well as for individual items within the scales, that you may want to think about.
4. Are there things about your scores that you feel good about? Are there things about your scores that you may want to consider changing?

---

when it leads to frustrations that seem insurmountable, rather than as a place to pause and reflect before making decisions, taking actions, and moving on.

Plateauing is becoming an important issue in educational organizations because of the demographics of our educational workforce. In many schools, the *average* professional experience of educators is between 14 and 16 years. This reality is important when we consider that it only takes 3 to 5 years to become a so-called expert (Bardwick, 1986). Compounding this problem is the fact that the educational workforce can be plotted on a bimodal curve—consisting of a large group of senior teachers and a growing number of newer teachers, with relatively few teachers at the midcareer stage. Recessionary times in the 1970s and the 1980s constrained many teachers from exercising the option to leave early in their careers. Declining enrollments aggravated the situation, holding down openings for new teachers.

This situation has changed rapidly as retirements reduce the number of senior educators in schools and increasing student enrollments add to the urgency to hire new teachers. But with a growing number of newer educators and relatively few midcareer educators, novices are, for the most part, learning how to play their roles from senior educators rather than from those closer to them in the career cycle. If many senior educators are plateaued, guess what newer teachers will learn? Encouraging and support-

> As I grow older, I pay less attention to what men say. I just watch what they do.
> —Andrew Carnegie

ing a resilient educational workforce means putting more of our energies into ensuring that the senior educator group is not characterized by symptoms of plateauing. If we are unwilling to do this, we will find newer educators replicating negative attitudes and behaviors.

> Man is what he believes.
> —Anton Chekhov

Strategies to Improve Educator Resiliency

Two ways of thinking about strategies for improvement of educator resiliency are suggested in the next section. First, we briefly focus on building individuals' internal and environment protective factors. Second, we explore the six resiliency factors in more detail to identify ways of responding to occupationally related barriers that affect resiliency and offer some strategies to overcome these barriers.

Focusing on Protective Factors

Chapter 1 included a summary of internal and environmental protective factors (Table 1.1). The more that both groups of factors are a part of our reality, the more we are likely to exhibit resilient behaviors. Internal factors, which are individually developed and enhanced by our unique experiences, affect how we relate to others, both at work and in our personal lives. But our ability to sustain our resiliency is directly affected by the extent to which environmental protective factors exist in our lives.

In other words, each of us develops and strengthens our internal protective factors in our own unique ways, but we do not do this in a vacuum:

> The general tendency of things throughout the world is to render mediocrity the ascendant power among mankind.
> —John Stuart Mill

The internal protective factors that support our resiliency are affected by the environments we live in. The reverse is also true: The extent to which we are able to display resilient behaviors can have negative or positive effects on our environments, one of the most important of which is our workplace, where we spend the majority of our waking hours.

We need to focus on the dynamic interplay that occurs between educators and their work environments and improve the resiliency-building capacity of these environments if we expect to enhance the resiliency of these professionals. The challenge is to create and maintain schools that promote professional growth, encourage achievement, and recognize exceptional efforts that focus on optimism and hopefulness rather than on pessimism and helplessness. This will require risk taking and creativity as well as will power to resist the criticism of naysayers.

Exercise 4.3 allows you to assess your own environment.

EXERCISE 4.3. Protective Factors and Educators at Your School

This exercise can be pursued by individuals or by groups. Groups are preferable if members are ready to explore educator resiliency at your school. Distribute Handout 2 (Table 1.1) to group members.

1. Approximately what percentage of the educators in your school exhibits a healthy level of the internal protective factors listed on Handout 2? How do you think these educators have achieved this healthy level of internal protective factors?
2. Which internal protective factors are most evident among your school's staff members? Why do you think these factors are most evident?
3. Are there any implications for needed changes on the part of the staff?
4. Next, review the list of environmental protective factors listed on Handout 2. Which of these factors do you think are most characteristic of your school environment? Why? Which is least characteristic of your school environment? Why?
5. Once again, are there any implications for needed changes on the part of the staff?

Overcoming Barriers to Educator Resiliency

Many specific environmentally related barriers to educator resiliency are of our own making. That is, they are embedded in the ways we structure our schools. It may be challenging, but we created these situations, and it is within our power to modify them in ways that are more supportive of educator resiliency.

What are these barriers? What strategies can we use to reduce them? We have organized the discussion of barriers and strategies around the six factors on the Resiliency Wheel (Figure 1.2 in Chapter 1) to encourage creative ways of thinking about improving educator resiliency. For each factor, we summarize the most relevant barriers and offer strategies for improvement. We encourage you and your colleagues to particularize and otherwise modify the suggested strategies to fit your own school's realities. In addition, please add others that might be worth considering in your situation.

Increase Prosocial Bonding

There are two barriers that are frequently identified as inhibitors of prosocial bonding among educators in schools. First, educators spend their workdays in isolation from other adults. Educators' efforts and time are devoted to working with youngsters, leaving little time for adult-to-adult interactions. Furthermore, the little interaction time that does exist for bonding tends to be misused, leading to distancing rather than closeness. For example, informal interactions that take place in teachers' lounges often center on discussing students' shortcomings, complaining about working conditions, and gossiping. Even when school staffs come together as formal groups, it is usually for meetings that are limited to brief periods of time and built around agendas (if indeed there are any!) that are set by the principal. Most of the time, such meetings do little to promote togetherness. Instead, they tend to be one-way communication sessions, with little time devoted to collegial exploration, decision making, and feedback. Given these barriers—work performance isolation, infrequent educator face-to-face interactions, and the misuses of even that minimal time—it is unrealistic to expect much prosocial bonding to take place.

Second, role performance evaluation is almost totally based on individual efforts. It rarely includes evaluation of cooperative group or team efforts. What matters regarding judgment of an educator's worth is how well specific professional roles are performed. As noted, in most schools, these roles are conducted in isolation. For example, teacher evaluations are traditionally focused on individually managed goals related to student achievement, safety, and security in the classroom. Cooperative efforts, such as involvement on site-based management teams, are not often given serious consideration in formal evaluations. In other words, although working cooperatively can promote bonding, there are few, if any, built-in organizational rewards to promote such activities. In fact, there are more likely to be disincentives because doing things cooperatively takes time away from individual role efforts, which is what counts most for evaluation purposes.

Strategies for Increasing Prosocial Bonding

The nature of the task, educating students, places major constrictions on opportunities for educator bonding, but there are ways of improving the situation. For example,

- Promote team-teaching efforts and other teaming activities (e.g., curriculum development groups) to encourage bonding. Adult teams can also model and make cooperative learning more relevant for students.

- Practice learning community principles that emphasize the value of everyone's contributions and capabilities. This can be promoted through a variety of means, including site-based management teams; study group; instructional and curricular demonstrations and presentations; visitations to other schools; and encouraging teachers to participate in state, regional, and national professional conferences and then sharing what they learned with their colleagues.

- Bring the school staff together to discuss, clarify, and update the school's vision, mission, and goals. This activity can support a shared sense of purpose and a stronger sense of community.

- Experiment with opportunities for the staff to share ideas and lend support to each other. For example, senior teachers can act as mentors.

- Develop and promote norms that promote cooperation and support. Norms such as collegial classroom coverage, peer feedback, and interpersonal support and recognition can lead to positive improvements in behaviors and relationships.

- Improve the way meetings are managed so they focus on meaningful issues and, when appropriate, provide opportunities for open discussion and consensus decision making.

Record other strategies that can increase prosocial bonding for educators:

- _____
  _____
- _____
  _____
- _____
  _____

Set Clear and Consistent Boundaries

Educators frequently live split lives when it comes to boundary setting. They have wide latitude to set boundaries within their specific roles, but they are not given much voice in decision making about expectations for their own conduct outside of their specific roles. For example, teachers establish many of the policies, rules, and expec-

> I am the decisive element in the classroom. . . . In all situations it is my response that decides whether a crisis will be escalated or de-escalated and a child humanized or dehumanized.
> —Haim Ginott

tations regarding behavioral boundaries for students in their classrooms. However, beyond the classroom, policies, rules, and expectations are usually set by the principal, superintendent, or other central office administrators and the school board. To one degree or another, the same high boundary-setting control within one's role and low boundary-setting control outside of one's role holds true for other educators, including diagnosticians, counselors, supervisors, and administrators.

Policies, rules, and expectations can vary from minutely detailed to vague and confusing, from consistently stated and enforced to arbitrary and contradictory, from logical to illogical, and from equitably applied or capricious and differentially applied. Many expectations are not even verbalized or put in writing, remaining as vaguely understood norms that emerge from the organizational culture and that are learned only through experience.

Strategies for Promoting Clear and Consistent Boundaries

> There is no conflict between liberty and safety. We will have both or neither.
>
> —Ramsey Clark

Growth, creativity, and achievement are important aspects of resiliency, but if these things are to occur, one first has to feel secure. This requires knowing the rules of the game, understanding their relevance and appropriateness, and believing that you can influence them. Strategies for creating healthy boundaries include these:

- Involve educators in establishing, interpreting, and implementing policies and rules. If they participate in these boundary-setting processes, they will more likely understand, accept, and support them.

- Communicate policies and rules clearly and frequently. This should be done in writing and checked to avoid misinterpretations.

- Make sure that norms are clarified, understood, and shared. Periodic clarification of norms, by updating and discussing them, can keep these expectations clear. Most important, it can help new staff members become acquainted with them without undue efforts.

Record other strategies that can promote clear and consistent boundaries for educators:

- _____
  _____
- _____
  _____
- _____
  _____

Teach Life Skills

> Life is what happens to us while we are making other plans.
> —Thomas La Mance

> We are made to persist. That's how we find out who we are.
> —Tobias Wolff

Many challenges confront educators who try to keep up with the skills required to do their jobs. First, preservice training, even if it is adequate at the time it is experienced, soon becomes outdated because of the increasingly complex tasks educators are asked to perform. Second, we live in a period of rapid change, marked by an explosion of technological breakthroughs, most of which impinge on what we do and how we do it in schools. Third, there are rarely sufficient resources—money, expertise, or time—to provide the enrichment opportunities that are needed to upgrade educators' life skills. The bottom line is that educators need to keep honing their skills to be able to provide the life skills growth opportunities that their students need.

Strategies for Fostering Life Skills

Life skill development has always been important for educators but is especially important now because there are so many senior members in our educational workforce. We need to provide opportunities for educators to learn and upgrade their skills, especially those with long-term service, if we want them to function effectively and be able to promote life skills for students in times of significant change. Strategies to consider include the following:

- Broaden the definition and scope of professional development. Frequently, professional development offerings are narrowly designed around role-related information and skills. However, life skills transcend role requirements. They are important for educators to

> Show me a thoroughly satisfied man—and I will show you a failure.
> —*Thomas Alva Edison*

  learn so they can carry out their responsibilities and, just as important, so they can enhance their students' life skills. Goal setting, problem solving, conflict management, and communications are examples of life skills that need to be learned, updated, and practiced by educators. In fact, if we view educators as whole persons with the potential for growth and development, rather than just as role holders, and support their potential as fully as possible, professional development can be defined even more broadly. For example, it might include learning about avocational interests and practices related to health enhancement.

- Survey your school's educational workforce about what *they think they need* in the way of professional development initiatives and activities. This may require a major shift in thinking away from central office to site-based and individual educator decision making about professional development.

- Practice adult learning principles. Educators need to be engaged in life skills development in ways that are consistent with what we know about adult learning. This includes positive focus on improvement; alternative learning opportunities based on individually defined needs; active engagement in problem solving, trust, respect, collaboration, and interaction; continuity; integration; and follow-up.

> The art of teaching is the art of assisting discovery.
> —*Mark Van Doren*

- Provide needed resources and create more on-the-job time for professional development opportunities. Many school districts recognize the need to add days to the school year contract for this purpose, but they usually lag far behind the business sector in the money and time made available and reserved for professional development. Some school districts are effectively searching for means to provide these necessary resources from within their local budgets, as well as from state and federally funded programs and private philanthropic sources. But finding time for this important activity is also necessary. Prioritization of time for professional development can send a powerful and positive message to the school's educators.

- Encourage exceptional educators from your school who have demonstrated their capability to apply important life skills effectively to share these skills. For example, they can team with faculty members from the local university to enrich preservice teacher preparation programs. At least two important benefits can be achieved through such an arrangement. First, novice teachers who are prepared by exceptional educators at the outset of their careers will be more likely to form good life skills and habits and practice them successfully than if they learn them later in their careers. Second, positive recognition and meaningful rewards can be gained by educators from your school district who participates in these activities.

Record other strategies that can foster life skills for educators:

- _____
  _____
- _____
  _____
- _____
  _____

Provide Caring and Support

Nurturing youngsters is a demanding task. It requires an enormous amount of energy and a seemingly endless supply of care and support. Most educators are nurturers by nature, but they can not give year after year without having their own needs for care and support met. Like our car batteries, educators need regular recharging if they are going to have the energy to support students' needs.

> We must have . . . a place where children can have a whole group of adults they can trust.
> —Margaret Mead

However, there are barriers that stand in the way of educators receiving sufficient care and support. First, there is not much time available for adult-to-adult interactions. Second, even the little time that is available is often squandered on negative criticism of students, teachers, and administrators rather than on positive, supportive feedback about efforts and achievements. Third, teacher evaluation is usually done "by the book"— the minimal number of visits required by the contract and focused on improvements needed much more than on supportive feedback that celebrates positive efforts and achievements. Furthermore, these evaluations are almost always done by administrators with little, if any, collegial teacher-to-teacher input. In short, many schools' working conditions do little to support the development of caring and support among educators.

Strategies for Enhancing Caring and Support

Demonstrations of caring and support are critical cornerstones for self-worth, connectedness, and belonging. This is particularly important now because many members of the current educational workforce have served a long time and have, too often, gotten little positive response, extrinsically or intrinsically, for their efforts. Some strategies that can change the situation include the following:

> Kind words can be short and easy to speak, but their echoes are truly endless.
> —Mother Teresa

- Provide purposeful and regular feedback that sends messages of caring and support. This behavior, if practiced regularly and sincerely among colleagues, as well as by administrators, can improve self-perceptions and promote the belief that one's role is important and, if performed well, is helpful and appreciated by other adults in the school. Administrators can be helpful if they heed Peters and Waterman (1982) who encourage "management by walking around," getting out and around in the school as frequently as possible so leaders know what is happening and can provide empathetic, supportive feedback based on observed behaviors.

> The race advances only by the extra achievements of the individual. You are the individual.
> —Charles Towne

- Create and support special events that recognize and celebrate educators' efforts. These symbolic events send the message that what educators do is important and appreciated. This is especially true when colleagues recognize each other's challenges and are supportive of each other's efforts and achievements.

- Establish a "sunshine" committee to ensure that members' life events, such as birthdays, marriages, sicknesses, and family activities, are recognized. Schools that have such committees and use them wisely have found them to be an effective way of demonstrating care and support.

- Discourage negative criticism and encourage positive regard and support for educators on the part of the community (and vice versa!). For example, provide information to the local newspaper about good things that are happening at the school and who the individuals are who are responsible for doing them.

> Faults are thick where love is thin.
> —James Howell

- Establish a community-school appreciation day that brings the broader community into the school for activities that focus on positive support and shared feedback.

Record other strategies that can enhance care and support for educators:

- _____
  _____
- _____
  _____
- _____
  _____

Set and Communicate High Expectations

In most school districts, the dominant message is, "Don't rock the boat," when it should be "Go for it!" "Don't rock the boat" is the message that administrators send teachers when they prioritize maintaining order over taking risks and challenging students to grow and achieve. It is also the message teachers get from their unions and associations when these organizations emphasize the need for unity and for behaving within agreed-on boundaries (i.e., "don't be a rate buster") rather than emphasizing the need for individual members to take initiatives and do all they can to achieve meaningful goals. The impact of such messages is compounded by the demotivating reality of the matrix-based salary compensation formula: One's salary is formulated on the basis of number of years of service and academic hours and degrees obtained, not the quality of one's role performance!

> You cannot teach and empower children to be successful if you do not hold yourself to be so. Everything you are and all that you believe is transmitted to your students at some level.

Strategies to Strengthen High Expectations

The extrinsic reward system in education does little to recognize or support individual efforts. Frequent messages of minimal expectations are also significant deterrents to creating high expectations. Here are some strategies that can counteract these barriers:

- Encourage regular feedback from colleagues, as well as from formal leaders, that show appreciation for efforts and recognition of achievements.
- Involve educators in the development and clarification of the school's mission, vision, and goals to promote a sense of purpose and expectations for achievement. If educators participate in defining these expectations, they are more likely to be enthused about them and understand how they can contribute to their achievement.

Given the isolating nature of most educators' work roles, it is important to bring them together often for goal clarification and for member motivation to achieve goals.

> I know well what I am fleeing from but not what I am in search of.
> —*Michel de Montaigne*

- Explore ways of reducing the isolation associated with educator role performance. Encouraging regular professional interactions can be quite helpful in this regard. For example, promoting team teaching and cooperative efforts to accomplish special projects can mitigate against role isolation. Similarly, job sharing and job expansion can be challenging to individual educators, support cooperative efforts, and promote schoolwide achievement.

> Is not life a hundred times too short for us to bore ourselves?
> —*Friedrich Nietzsche*

- Maximize on-task time by reducing the extent of low priority maintenance activities (e.g., filling out extensive federal, state, and district forms). This can send the message that the organization's leaders will do what they can to help educators focus their time on helping students achieve positive educational outcomes.

- Modify extrinsic reward systems to emphasize achievement and recognition of individual efforts. Given the deeply embedded reality of the matrix system and of union protection of their members, it is not likely that this constraint on high expectations will ever be fully removed. However, there are ways of modifying the problem. For example, grants can be awarded to teachers to develop innovative teaching units; extra pay can be awarded to teachers who are able and willing to help students in need of support outside of regular school hours; and funds can be reserved for professional development opportunities, including tuition for courses at local universities or travel money for educators, who are identified by their peers as making important contributions to the school, to attend local, regional, and national educational conferences.

Record other strategies that can strengthen high expectations for educators:

- _____
  _____
- _____
  _____
- _____
  _____
- _____
  _____
- _____

Provide Opportunities for Meaningful Participation

A life spent in making mistakes is not only more honorable but more useful than a life spent in doing nothing.
—George Bernard Shaw

As educators proceed through career stages, they become more knowledgeable and skilled about their specific work roles. Once they achieve role competence, many of them seek new challenges. They may make mistakes, but they recognize that opportunities for growth and development are vital to their well-being. One way for them to grow is to participate more broadly in organizational life in ways that transcend the requirements of their assigned roles. Many seek these experiences because they want to be part of something bigger than they are and give something back to the organizations they serve. It also is stimulated by the adult learner's need to grow and take on new challenges.

There is no meaning to life except the meaning man gives his life by the unfolding of his powers.
—Erich Fromm

The problem is that there are not sufficient opportunities to participate meaningfully in broad-scale activities because educators' roles are usually defined quite narrowly: Teachers teach, counselors counsel, and administrators administer. In addition, few career development opportunities are made available, so it is difficult for educators to change roles and explore alternative ways of participating. There are few promotion possibilities (e.g., as demonstration teachers or staff developers) *within* the teaching role, and the possibility of changing roles (e.g., becoming a diagnostician, counselor, or administrator) is limited by the flat hierarchy and the attendant low supervisor-supervisee ratios that typify our school systems. Furthermore, given resource constraints for professional development, especially in knowledge and skill areas beyond one's direct role, there are not enough opportunities to learn skills that are necessary for meaningful participation. For example, to effectively participate on site-based management teams, educators need to acquire basic team management skills. Even with skill development and the best of intentions, there is scant time available during the workday to contribute beyond daily role expectations.

Strategies for Improving Meaningful Participation

Educators need adult learning challenges, and school leaders need all the help they can get to accomplish their purposes. Therefore, it is important to focus on the development of opportunities to participate meaningfully. Some ways of going about this include the following:

- Practice site-based management approaches that promote participation by educators (as well as by community members and students). To promote educator participation, organizationwide responsibilities need to be built in as part of members' role expectations (e.g., participation on curricular and extracurricular committees and other schoolwide responsibility areas). But it is important that the focus be on things that are meaningful to participants. For example, discussing educational goals and curriculum development is more relevant to teachers than discussing the lunch menu and grounds maintenance. Motivation to participate in school-based decision making depends on whether there is a sense of value, or ownership, for the content of the discussion.

- Urge administrators to learn and practice facilitation skills for group participation in governance rather than taking sole responsibility for all schoolwide problem solving and decision making. This is a two-way street, of course. Administrators need to become more skilled and comfortable with being convenors and facilitators who invite others to join them in establishing a vision, agreeing on a mission and goals, and monitoring activities that support goal achievement. Likewise, teachers and other educators need to be willing to take on schoolwide tasks.

- Promote team planning and team teaching. Such cooperative efforts and role sharing can encourage the development of creative ideas and provide motivation to become more involved in meaningful activities.

- Promote participation by changing the way meetings are managed: for example, getting agendas out early so everyone can think about issues ahead of time; limiting the number of items on the agenda so there is more time for discussion; avoiding using valuable meeting time to share information that can be disseminated by other means; emphasizing consensus decision making; encouraging volunteerism for task accomplishment; and most important, ensuring that decisions lead to actions so members believe that their participation is important.

Record other strategies that can improve meaningful participation among educators:

- _____
  _____
- _____
  _____
- _____
  _____

Over time, you and others on your school's staff have probably given thought to the resiliency barriers discussed in this chapter. Exercise 4.4 can

EXERCISE 4.4. Responding to Educator Resiliency Barriers

1. Distribute the Barriers to Educator Resiliency sheet (Handout 9 in the Resource section) and lead a discussion about the barriers. Do members understand them? Do they seem to fit the situation at your school?

2. Divide the staff into six subgroups. Assign each group to a separate workstation. Put a piece of flip chart paper at each work station, with a different resiliency factor at the top of each sheet (i.e., prosocial bonding at the first station, boundary setting at the second, life skills at the third, caring and support at the fourth, high achievement at the fifth, and meaningful participation at the sixth).

3. Give each group about 5 minutes to review the barriers to the resiliency factor on their sheet of paper and briefly brainstorm ways of improving the situation at your school. A recorder should be assigned and asked to write the group's ideas on the chart paper.

4. Ask each group to pass its pages on to the next group, in a clockwise manner, so that there will be a new resiliency factor to explore at each workstation. Ask the groups to take about 5 minutes to first read the ideas that the previous group suggested and then add their own ideas. Then ask each group to pass its pages, clockwise, to the next group.

5. The idea-generating process should continue until every group has responded to all six factors on the chart paper. Then, pass the pages on one more time so that each group has the chart paper with the resiliency factor they worked on initially. The task is for each group to review *all* the ideas suggested regarding improving their particular factor. After the review, group members should discuss and agree on the overall ideas that have been suggested and list them at the bottom of the paper.

6. Recorders should take turns sharing the basic strategies that were identified. With further discussion and agreement by the large group, these strategies can become the basis for schoolwide action planning. Check to see if there is interest in implementing any of them. If there is, ask for thoughts about next steps.

be used as a means of encouraging the staff to share these thoughts and develop suggestions to overcome educator resiliency barriers.

School faculties can be motivated to institutionalize behaviors and beliefs that enhance resiliency for them as well as for their students. But they cannot do it alone. They need to work in schools that are organized in ways that promote student and faculty resiliency. In the next chapter, we will focus on schools and explore ways that they can be organized and managed that are more supportive of resiliency building for students, faculty, and community.

CHAPTER 5

School Resiliency

Creating Supportive Environments for Students, Educators, and Communities

At a gut level all of us know that much more goes into the process of keeping a large organization vital and responsive than the policy statements, new strategies, plans, budgets, and organization charts can possibly depict. But all too often we behave as though we don't know it. If we want change, we fiddle with the strategy. Or we change the structure. Perhaps the time has come to change our ways.

—Peters and Waterman (1982, p. 3)

Most schools do things right, but that is not the same as doing the right things (Bennis, 1989; Sergiovanni, 1990)! Schools are organizations with deeply embedded and strongly held belief systems about what should be done and how it should be done. When communities were sedentary and expectations were clearer and more predictable, it may have been sufficient to take a "business as usual" stance about purposes and how they should be pursued in our schools. But that will not suffice for the foreseeable future because challenge and change will be the dominant reality.

Schools need to be sensitive to community expectations and responsive to community demands. This is difficult enough to do when demands are clear and there is widespread agreement about what schools are supposed to do, but it becomes increasingly challenging when demands are unclear, intense, broad in

> An old error is always more popular than a new truth.
>
> —German proverb

scope, and often contradictory. In fact, in most communities, there is no longer a clear agreement about the role of the schools. Given this lack of clarity, school districts need to be *proactive—they must continuously reinvent themselves to meet changing realities.*

> There is nothing permanent except change.
> —Heraclitus

This chapter focuses on schools as organizations that, if they wish, can promote the resiliency of students and educators and become more accessible to and supportive of their surrounding communities. The chapter explores why changing the way a school functions is often quite difficult, suggests ways of planning for change, and provides strategies that can improve its potential to promote resiliency for students, educators, and communities. The chapter also provides some exercises that encourage readers to examine the status quo regarding their school's ability to support resiliency development.

Does Your School Support Resiliency?

A good place to begin is with an assessment of your school's current situation. Exercises 5.1, 5.2, and 5.3 are intended to help guide your group through this assessment. They relate and build on each other so, if time permits, ask the group to proceed through them in the order in which they are presented. This will help move the group toward shared understandings and agreements. Exercise 5.1 should help clarify your school's impact on student, educator, and community resiliency.

EXERCISE 5.1. Your School's Resiliency

In what ways does the school *promote* resiliency among students, educators, and community members? In what ways does the school *deter* resiliency among students, educators, and community members?

1. Ask members to complete the survey presented in Table 5.1 (Handout 10 in the Resource section).
2. Develop a composite score sheet for the group by making a large copy of Table 5.1 on a chalkboard or on chart paper and filling in members' scores. Compute the group's mean scores and put them in the "Overall" column.
3. Discuss the implications of the mean scores. What is the overall sense of the group regarding whether the school supports or deters resiliency?
4. Are there distinctive differences regarding the school's support of resiliency for students, educators, and community members? If there are differences, ask group members to discuss why they think they exist.
5. Last, ask group members to share the comments they wrote about the six resiliency factors. Check for the extent to which they agree about these comments.

TABLE 5.1 My School: Does It Deter or Support Resiliency Development?

1. The six resiliency factors are listed in the following table. If you need the definitions, refer to Chapter 1.
2. *To what extent does your school deter or support the development of the six resiliency factors among students, educators, and community members?* Use the following 5-point scale to record your judgment in each of the columns:

   Supports Resiliency 5 4 3 2 1 *Deters Resiliency*

3. Think about how the school does overall and record your judgment in the "Overall" column.
4. Add any comments you may want that support your judgments.

Resiliency Factors	Students	Educators	Community	Overall	Comments
Prosocial bonding					
Clear and consistent boundaries					
Life skills					
Caring and support					
High expectations					
Meaningful participation					

In all likelihood, the exercise and discussion will result in group perceptions that the school is doing better regarding some resiliency factors than it is with others, and perhaps, with some groups more than with other groups. The group may view the school as doing a good job of supporting everyone's resiliency, or it may view it as doing a poor job of promoting everyone's resiliency. Just as likely, the group may conclude that the school varies in its impact with each of the three groups. Every school situation is different. The important thing is to agree about yours.

EXERCISE 5.2. Beliefs About Schools and Resiliency

1. The following statements should be posted on a chalkboard or on a flip chart page:

   There is widespread belief that the school's role should be limited to teaching the basics and keeping youngsters academically engaged during their formative years.

   Or

   There is widespread understanding of the important role the school plays in developing youngsters' capacities to cope with life's challenges.

2. Ask the group to discuss which belief is most characteristic of your school. What are the implications for the school's ability to enhance student resiliency? What, if any, changes in beliefs need to be encouraged?

3. Next, post the following statements about the school and educator resiliency:

   Educators are viewed as professionals who are responsible for their own growth and development.

   Or

   There is recognition that educators need regular growth opportunities and that they must be role models of resiliency if we expect students to become resilient.

4. Ask the group to discuss which belief is most characteristic of your school, the implications of this belief, and whether any changes in beliefs need to be encouraged.

5. Post the following statements about the school and community member resiliency:

   The school views educating youngsters as its specific responsibility, and that this is best accomplished with minimal involvement by members of the community.

   Or

   There is a clear understanding that the larger community has an impact on the school's effectiveness, and the school welcomes community members' efforts to become involved in school life.

6. As in Step 4, ask the group to discuss which belief is most characteristic of the school, the implications of this belief, and whether any changes need to be encouraged.

7. Ask the group to synthesize the discussion. Does the school support student, educator, and community resiliency? Are other actions called for?

Does the group believe that your school needs to do more to promote resiliency more purposefully? Beliefs need to be clarified and agreed on if necessary changes are to be pursued. Exercise 5.2 can help group members clarify their beliefs, help promote reflection, and encourage them to become more sensitive about the importance of the role of the school in supporting the resiliency of everyone involved.

All schools are candidates for change in ways that can improve their capacities to promote resiliency. What matters most is to first recognize this potential and then take meaningful actions to help the school fulfill its potential. With perceptions and beliefs clarified, as suggested in Exercises 5.1 and 5.2, Exercise 5.3 can help the group clarify the school's current state of readiness to support members' resiliency.

EXERCISE 5.3. What Do We Do Well? Do Okay? Need to Start to Do?

How does the school promote resiliency? In what ways does it fall short? What else may need to be done to improve its resiliency-building capacity?

1. Ask group members to identify *what the school is presently doing well* to promote resiliency among students, educators, and community members. Encourage them to think broadly. For example, resiliency can be promoted through governance structures, policies and procedures, communications, instructional approaches, curriculum, and outreach efforts. Ask members to record their agreements on a chalkboard or on chart paper.
2. Next, ask group members to identify *what the school is doing "OK" but could do better to promote resiliency.* Again, encourage them to think broadly. List things they agree about on a chalkboard or chart paper. Ask the group to identify what needs to be changed or improved on to promote student, educator, and community resiliency.
3. Last, ask group members to identify *things they know about (or may have read about) that can promote resiliency but are not presently the way things are being done in the school.* After a list is generated, ask group members to prioritize suggestions. Which would be most likely to promote resiliency if they were to be introduced at the school?

(We encourage you to keep the three lists for later reference if the group decides to move ahead with resiliency improvement efforts.)

Improving School Resiliency Means Changing Schools

Once the group completes Exercises 5.1, 5.2, and 5.3, the picture should be clearer regarding beliefs about the school's current situation and changes that may be necessary. However, beliefs alone will not lead to a better tomorrow, even if there is agreement about the need for change, a sense of what needs to be done, and a game plan to bring about agreed-on changes.

> Man has a biological capacity
> for change. When this capacity
> is overwhelmed, the capacity is
> in future shock.
> —*Alvin Toffler*

Goodwill and readiness are important starting points, but, as anyone who has been involved in educational reform efforts knows, they probably are not sufficient. Barriers to change need to be confronted and overcome. Three barriers in particular are likely to be encountered:

> Traditionalists are pessimists
> about the future and
> optimists about the past.
> —*Lewis Mumford*

1. *Change means loss and destabilization.* Whether related to current beliefs and ideologies or practices and behaviors, change requires letting go of something. Change dissolves meaning as new purposes and processes are explored and put in place. It also represents uncertainty and the likelihood of some discomfort. Change requires risk taking as participants gain new knowledge and learn new roles and skills, all demanding extra efforts and trust in the unknown.

Individuals who are having a difficult time with the destabilization that accompanies change are often labeled *resistant*, an oversimplified label that can be dysfunctional.

2. *Change is confusing.* Enthusiasm dissipates quickly without clear purposes and strong support during the implementation process and confusion can take its place. When you try something new, you must define and communicate what you are doing. Further, it is one thing to declare a new direction, but quite another to make it happen, particularly without evidence of support in such forms as resources, public endorsements and waivers from key players.

3. *Change upsets power relationships.* Organizations are political systems [i.e., they are engaged with the acquisition and distribution of scarce resources, including funds, space, and time]. As such, shifts in the balance of power should be expected as a natural outcome of change, for reasons that have nothing to do with the content of the change itself. You must understand and manage power or else the power concerns that people have may negatively affect the outcomes of your change efforts. Those who have power based on status, roles, or control of resources may fear that they will lose their power. Similarly, those who do not have power may view the destabilization that accompanies change as an opportunity to gain it. (Milstein, 1993, pp. 43-44)

Loss and destabilization, confusion, and power relationship games are likely to be experienced in most any school change effort. They can be viewed negatively as insurmountable barriers or neutrally as normal realities of any organizational change. With a bit of creativity, they can even be viewed positively as the stuff from which school resiliency can be built. After all, resiliency is all about being able to bounce back from stressful, adverse situations! Exercise 5.4 should help members of your school community develop greater understanding and sensitivity about the dynamics of organizational change. It should also help them prepare for and be more realistic about planning to enhance the resiliency-building potential of the school.

EXERCISE 5.4. How Does Your School Cope With Organizational Change?

1. Ask group members to think about past change efforts at the school. The focus of these efforts might have been on governance, structure, instructional approaches, curriculum content, or any other school-related areas. Post situations that members identify on a chalkboard or on chart paper.
2. Ask the group to review the situations and pick one to explore that many of them have participated in or with which they are at least familiar.
3. Post the three change barriers identified earlier—loss and destabilization, confusion, and power relationships—on a chalkboard or on chart paper. Clarify them as needed.
4. Ask group members to share stories about the situations they selected. Did they experience these barriers?
5. If time permits, do the same activity for another change situation the group has identified.
6. Guided by the following questions, ask the group to draw conclusions from the discussion:
   a. Given the three barriers to change and their occurrence in past situations, are they likely to occur if efforts to enhance the resiliency-building capacity of the school are initiated?
   b. If so, what might be done to respond to them effectively?
7. Ask the group to synthesize and record their agreements so they can be referred to during future change initiatives.

There are things that we know about organizational change generally and about changing schools specifically. We need to consider the following to effectively respond to the barriers that are likely to be encountered as school resiliency-building initiatives are initiated:

Focus on leadership. Successful change requires committed and effective leadership to shape and communicate values, visions, and expectations. Those who lead such efforts need to role model expected behaviors, support and reward those who participate, and keep the focus on purposes. The emphasis should be on *the function of leadership,* not on *leaders per se,* to encourage shared responsibility and initiative taking and to promote members' resiliency as they take responsibility and engage in change.

> Leadership is *action,* not position.
> —*Donald H. McGannon*

Change perspectives by changing the culture of the school. People's behaviors and actions are affected by the culture of the organization, which can be defined as "the *norms* that inform people about what is acceptable and what is not, the dominant *values* that the organization cherishes above others [and] the *basic assumptions and beliefs* that are shared by members" (Owens, 1991, p. 28). School cultures are most frequently characterized by a focus on conformity, rules, discipline, and regularity. In such school cultures, motivation for growth and risk taking are likely to be in short supply. Rather, they are more likely to be marked by high absenteeism, low participation in schoolwide activities, minimal parental involvement, negative talk and judgmental labeling in educators' lounges, teachers leaving immediately at the end of the school day, poor building maintenance, and a heavy emphasis on rules and penalties.

> The perpetual obstacle to human advancement is custom.
> —John Stuart Mill

Changing such maintenance-oriented cultures requires shifting perspectives. This includes modifying the culture by shifting the focus:

- From doing things right to doing the right things
- From isolation and individualism to cooperation, teamwork, and relationships
- From behaving reactively to behaving proactively
- From catching members doing something wrong to catching members doing something right
- From quick-fix solutions to broad-based, long-term responses to complex problems
- From viewing innovative efforts that fall short as "failures" to viewing them as learning opportunities that are part of most any significant change efforts.

Build capabilities and confidence by providing skill development. Skill development is as important for successful change as it is for the promotion of resiliency. A good beginning place might be to provide opportunities to obtain relevant information about strategies that promote resiliency. Building on this knowledge base, opportunities can be provided to learn and practice facilitation skills that are needed to implement resiliency-promoting behaviors (e.g., goal setting, conflict management, communications, and decision making.)

We use the term *skill development* rather than *professional development* because we believe that this activity should be made available to *all* participants, not just educators. If students, educators, and community members are to participate effectively as partners, status differentials must be minimized and skill development must be provided.

Emphasize the way things will stay the same as well as the way things will change. Continuity is a necessary foundation for security. This is particularly true when we are asked to make significant changes. Individuals will more likely have the confidence to take necessary risks if they believe that there will be sufficient continuity, that known points of reference will be maintained regularly and meaningfully. In other words, that a balance between security and risk taking will be promoted.

Resiliency development is a change that is particularly well suited to promoting continuity because *it is about changing our approach to our work, not about changing the work itself.* That is, resiliency is an attitude, a state of mind, about how to behave in learning communities. With this understanding in place, attitudinal changes that may be required for the school to become more supportive of resiliency are not likely to be so disorienting to group members.

> The art of progress is to preserve order amid change and to preserve change amid order.
>
> —Alfred North Whitehead

Monitor progress. Even the best-laid plans can go astray. Keeping on course toward agreed-on goals requires regular and meaningful assessment of progress (see Chapter 7). But strategic adjustments that are needed can only be made if there are clear and agreed-on goals and good assessment measures are developed to monitor the extent to which they are being achieved. Assessment efforts can also help to maintain commitment and motivation. If participants see results, they are more likely to have a sense of achievement and to continue making positive contributions.

Backwards Planning

It is one thing to believe that a school should be reconfigured in ways that promote resiliency for all members, but it is quite another to move the organization in ways that make this a reality. To support this goal, we suggest an approach that can help you and others at the school become clearer about what needs to be changed and how to go about changing it—backwards planning.

Backwards planning emphasizes the importance of agreeing about the vision you hope to create before making decisions and taking actions. What should your resilient school of tomorrow look like? Exercise 5.5 can help the group clarify school goals that can lead to increased support for the resiliency of its members. With end goals in mind, plans can be developed to bring them about.

EXERCISE 5.5. A Backwards Planning Activity: Take the Roof Off the School

Ask group members to respond to the following statement: *It is now 5 years into the future, 5 years since efforts were started to improve the resiliency-building capacity of your school. Changes have been difficult to implement, but most everyone believes that the effort has been highly successful. What does "success" look like?*

1. Ask group members to imagine they are hovering over the school. Ask them to imagine that they are able to take the roof off of the school and peer down to see what is going on in it. What do they believe they will see 5 years from now in their more resilient school? For example, what kinds of interactions will be going on? What will classrooms and other areas of the school look like? What will be displayed on the walls? Ask group members to share their images. As they do, post them on a chalkboard or on chart paper.
2. Ask the group to review the posted images. Encourage them to clarify and modify the images and add any others that might be useful.
3. Share the six resiliency factors (see Figure 1.2) with the group. Ask members to check their list of images against the six factors. Are all of the resiliency factors adequately addressed by their list? If not, ask members to think of things they want to add to their lists, especially for those factors that may be absent or underrepresented.
4. Last, ask the group to identify the major delineating characteristics of the school as it becomes more supportive of resiliency. Review the agreements, and ask the group to develop goal statements that reflect what they want to achieve. Post the agreements and the goals. Save them for future reference.

Exercise 5.5 was expanded from Henderson and Milstein (1996).

Knowing where you want to be and agreeing on the vision or what it will look like can be a powerful starting place for getting there! Backwards planning is an approach that starts with agreements about preferred futures. With this vision in mind, it is easier to state goals and then to identify strategies that can support them, as well as when these strategies should be introduced and pursued.

School Resiliency-Building Strategies

> So much of what we call management consists in making it difficult for people to work.
> —Peter Drucker

School leaders often unconsciously inhibit growth and development for adult members, as well as for students. Although each school is unique, there are common organizationally based dynamics that cut across school levels, school districts, and geographic locations. Understanding these dynamics and responding to them effectively by modifying attitudes, structures, and behaviors in ways that are supportive of resiliency development can make a positive difference for students, educators, and the community.

We next discuss the organizationally based dynamics that need to be considered when promoting each of the six resiliency factors. We also offer some strategies for responding to them in ways that can improve the situation. We encourage you and your group to modify and add to these suggestions to meet the particular needs of your school situation.

Increase Prosocial Bonding

Bonding is more likely to be promoted if the school's climate and culture are supportive. Organizational climate, like the weather, can be a major challenge to basic survival if it is cold and foreboding. It can also be a major strategy for community building and bonding if it is warm and sunny. A school's culture is less observable, but it can have an even greater impact on resiliency building. Some organizational cultures promote status differences and foster the kinds of behavior that lead to distrust, inhibit connectedness and teaming, and promote fear and reprisals. Other organization cultures promote empowerment and equality, encourage learning and growth, and recognize individual and group accomplishments. Cultures change slowly because they are so deeply embedded over long periods of time, but with focused attention and patience, they can be positively affected.

> A school can create a "coherent" environment, a climate, more potent than any single influence—teachers, class, family, neighborhood—so potent that for at least six hours a day it can override almost everything else in the lives of children.
>
> —Ron Edmonds

Strategies for Increasing Prosocial Bonding

Efforts to modify and strengthen the school's climate and culture can positively affect members' bonding. Some places to start include these:

- Model and encourage respect, cooperation, support, and trust. These behaviors promote positive relationships and can send a powerful message: People are important and their well-being should be an organizational priority.
- Encourage members to discuss and craft organizational vision and mission statements or to review and modify them as needed if they already exist. This exercise can stimulate the process of organizational change and promote resiliency by emphasizing and clarifying shared values, shifting resource allocation priorities, and institutionalizing important governance, structural, and educational modifications.

- Emphasize cooperation, teaming, and support whenever possible. Many ways to do these things have already been suggested in the book.

Record other strategies that can increase prosocial bonding at your school:

- _____
  _____
- _____
  _____
- _____
  _____

Set Clear and Consistent Boundaries

School boundaries exist in two forms—(a) policies and rules that are formalized and (b) norms that informally shape behavioral expectations. Boundaries are necessary because students, educators, staff, and community members need to know how they should interact to accomplish given ends. There is no problem with boundaries if they are reasonable, understood, and supported. But if they are capricious, inconsistent, unclear, or arbitrarily developed by a few rule makers for many others, they can be serious impediments to members' resiliency. For example, *students* can easily become alienated from the school if the rules are perceived to be unreasonable or unfair. In fact, if this happens, they may turn to peer-developed norms, which are likely to promote behaviors that directly challenge those fostered by school policies and rules. *Educators and staff* usually have wide latitude for rule setting as they affect their own roles, but frequently, they do not have much control over behavioral expectations outside of their domains. This control dichotomy can lead to confusion and frustration. *Community members* are typically confronted by formal and informal rule structures at the school that are not of their own making and that often send a clear and negative message: "Stay out unless we ask you to come in!"

> Integrity has no need of rules.
>
> —*Albert Camus*

Strategies for Promoting Clear and Consistent Boundaries

> The fact, in short, is that *freedom to be meaningful in an organized society must consist of an amalgam of hierarchy of freedoms and restraints.*
>
> —*Samuel Hendel*

If boundaries are clear and "owned" by school members, everyone knows how they should behave, and they can then concentrate on teaching, learning, relating, and cooperating. If they feel safe and secure, they can take the required risks to grow and develop. Feeling safe and secure can be promoted by the following:

- Clarify the school's vision, mission, and goals so that everyone understands purposes and priorities.
- Share behavioral expectations with staff, students, families, and others from the community, and encourage positive behaviors that can, over time, be embedded intrinsically.
- Clarify role expectations and the ways roles relate, and provide opportunities to give voice to questions and concerns.
- Base rules and policies on research, information gathering, and best practices.
- Provide regular opportunities for members to review, modify, and otherwise update the policies and rules that affect them.
- Follow through to ensure that equitable schoolwide implementation of agreed-on boundaries occurs.

Record other strategies that can promote boundary setting for your school:

- _____
  _____
- _____
  _____
- _____
  _____

Teach Life Skills

Schools that narrowly focus on academic basics and are preoccupied with maintenance tasks, such as budgets and books, miss extraordinary opportunities to support the development of student, educator, staff, and community members' life skills. Schools need to take a comprehensive perspective about their roles in life skill development, one that views all participants as members of learning communities. Learning communities are concerned with *all* of the growth needs of *all* members, not just *some* of the growth needs of *some* members.

Strategies for Fostering Life Skills

Strategies that can promote members' life skills include these:

- Leaders model expectations for life skill development and send consistent messages that change and renewal are necessary for all members of the learning community, as well as for the survival of the school itself. Leaders model these expectations when they practice and promote positive problem finding, diagnosis, decision making, problem solving, conflict management, and intervention and change practices and when they make efforts to monitor and evaluate outcomes. Involving students, faculty, and community members in these activities can provide unique opportunities for participation, learning, and growth.

- Respond to challenges from students, staff, parents, and other community members proactively and creatively rather than reactively and defensively, openly rather than guardedly, and seek feedback rather than cut off their inputs.

- Provide opportunities for all members' skill development in areas such as critical thinking, effective problem solving, and conflict management so they can participate in schoolwide improvement efforts effectively and with confidence.

- Encourage such cooperative efforts as consensus decision making, goal setting, and teaming for organizational improvement. Learning these life skills as a group promotes commitment and motivation to practice them as a group. As an added bonus, once learned, these life skills will likely become part of the ongoing repertoire of those who participate.

Record other strategies that can foster life skills at your school:

- _____
  _____

- _____
  _____

- _____
  _____

Provide Caring and Support

> He could pass by virtue all his life and never stumble over it, but his nose smelled out neither side of human nature as instinctively as a bird smells manure.
>
> —*Irving Stone*

Schools vary along a continuum from places where control is emphasized and members feel isolated and alienated to places where inclusion is emphasized and members feel connected, cared for, and supported. Schools that emphasize control believe that regimented daily routines, compliance, and micromanagement of resources are required because students, educators, and community members will not otherwise cooperate or participate positively. These are schools that need to put more focus on their members' care and support and less focus on compliance.

Strategies for Enhancing Caring and Support

To promote care and support, it is important to institutionalize helpful strategies:

- Develop school climates that emphasize positive feedback and co-operation, as well as caring.

- Appoint school leaders who understand the need to be a regular presence throughout the school, promoting care and support, rather than spending most of the school day in their offices. Leaders who roam the building, speak regularly and by name to students and staff, welcome community members, respond to members' concerns, and reach out to students' families send powerful messages that care and support are highly valued in the school.

> Kindness in words creates confidence. Kindness in thinking creates profoundness. Kindness in giving creates love.
>
> —Lao-tzu

- Avoid favoritism and distribute resources equitably to demonstrate that there is concern for the well-being and growth of *all* members.

- Shift the emphasis from external control of members' behaviors to an emphasis on shared values, norms, and expectations. In the process, a community of learners, encompassing all members, will be promoted. Through frank and open exchanges, members can come to understand each other better, empathize with each other's needs, and view each other as respected partners rather than distrusted competitors.

- Celebrate members' rites of passages, including student progress and achievements, staff members' professional accomplishments and career development initiatives, and community members' support and contributions to the school.

- Publicize members' efforts to reach out and help, for instance, by serving on schoolwide committees and recognizing others who make similar contributions to the school. Making note of these outreach activities sends messages that such acts are highly valued.

Record other strategies that can enhance caring and support in your school:

- _____
  _____
- _____
  _____
- _____
  _____
- _____
  _____
- _____
  _____

Set and Communicate High Expectations

> A subject for a great poet would be God's boredom after the seventh day of Creation.
>
> —Friedrich Nietzsche

Schools function like the worst stereotypes of organizational bureaucracies when they focus on meeting minimal performance expectations and producing minimally acceptable outcomes rather than on encouraging exceptional performance expectations and producing extraordinary outcomes. Such schools are places noted for competing forces that require bargaining and trade-offs rather than places noted for supportive and symbiotic forces that build on each other in ways that promote win-win opportunities and high achievement. Worst of all, the focus is on defending and preserving rather than on taking risks and creating.

This mentality can lead to school dynamics that depress the basic human desire for challenge and growth. Such schools are places where:

1. *Students* get messages that they need only meet minimal standards to pass on to the next grade.
2. *Educators* get little positive feedback, extrinsic rewards are limited to lockstep salary schedules, and are often required to participate in professional development activities that do not take their own perceived needs for growth into consideration.
3. *Community members* are told that they should not "interfere" in school matters.

The potential for mediocre performance, as well as a lack of self-confidence, is great in such schools.

Strategies for Strengthening High Expectation:

The following strategies can foster high expectations:

> I believe that anyone can conquer fear by doing the things he fears to do, provided he keeps doing them until he gets a record of successful experiences behind him.
>
> —Eleanor Roosevelt

- Permeate the school with "can do" messages. Norms need to change from acceptance of nonengagement, minimal effort, and low expectations to norms of support for achievement. "You *can* do it, and I will support your efforts to do it!" is a message that may need to be stimulated initially by the school's leaders, but if it is to take hold, it needs to be believed and practiced by everyone—students, educators, staff, and community members.

- Encourage goal setting and achievement for everyone. This can be pursued in many ways. For example, school leaders can set the tone by making sure that the school's vision, mission, and goals are translated into meaningful operational plans with clearly established responsibilities and time lines. Teachers can prepare annual professional development plans and share them with their colleagues and administrators. Parents and students, as noted in Chapter 3, can contract with teachers to establish and accomplish learning expectations. Parents and other community members can be asked to participate in site-based governance activities and to volunteer their time and talents to school and classroom improvement efforts. Given appropriate challenges and sufficient support, risk taking, and experimentation, everyone can experience meaningful achievements.

> The mind, once expanded to
> The dimension of larger ideas,
> Never returns to its
> Original size
> —Oliver Wendell Holmes

> If at first you don't succeed,
> you're running about average.
> —M. H. Alderson

- Monitor progress and achievements regularly. Conducted properly, monitoring can send clear messages that everyone's success matters. Supportive feedback for efforts that are made and suggestions for improvement can help promote success.

> Treat people as if they were what they ought to be and you help them to become what they are capable of being.
> —Johann W. von Goethe

- Encourage learning opportunities that legitimize giving and receiving help. With such encouragement and some practice, fear and distrust will begin to subside. As members cooperate and support each other, they will become more involved and more encouraging of everyone's success.

- Celebrate achievements and tell stories about "heroes"—students, educators, staff, and community members—who, with support, focus, and motivation, have overcome the odds to succeed in school and in life.

> We are told that talent creates its own opportunities. But it sometimes seems that intense desire creates not only its own opportunities, but its own talents.
> —Eric Hoffer

Record other strategies that can strengthen high expectations for your school:

- _____
  _____
- _____
  _____
- _____
  _____

Provide Opportunities for Meaningful Participation

There is growing recognition that widespread involvement in site-based decision making is important. All participants, students, educators, and community members alike, have concerns, ideas, and energies that are relevant and can contribute to the school's success. As they get opportunities to participate in schoolwide agendas, they will extend their own resiliency. However, they will only be motivated to contribute to school improvement efforts if their participation is valued in discussions and in decision making.

> A school should not be a preparation for life. A school should be life.
>
> —Elbert Hubbard

Unfortunately, for several reasons, widespread participation in school affairs is not usually promoted. First, site-based activities are often pro forma and micromanaged by administrators rather than relevant and open equitably to all participants. Some administrators limit participation because they are uncomfortable about sharing authority, particularly if they are going to be held responsible for outcomes that they do not control. Other administrators may understand and support involvement and participation but may lack the facilitation skills that are required (e.g., goal setting, conflict management, and team development).

Second, many educators think of students, parents, and other community members as clients or customers to be served rather than as legitimate and important partners and participants in the process.

Third, teacher involvement in schoolwide decision making has proved to be an illusive goal in many schools. In part, this is because schoolwide problem solving and decision making has traditionally been viewed as the prerogative and responsibility of administrators. But it is also due, in part, to teachers' preparation and experience, which is mainly limited to classroom-level curriculum and instruction. These activities are usually performed individually and in isolation from others, which is a situation that does not foster group skills or encourage cooperative efforts.

Fourth, there is a paucity of meaningful rewards or even recognition for students, teachers, parents, and other community members who participate in schoolwide problem solving and improvement efforts. Besides the absence of positive motivation to participate, such contributions require time and effort that is simply added to everything else that must still be done. In short, participating is likely to drain energy away from members' primary interests and responsibilities.

Strategies to Improve Meaningful Participation

Moving toward more meaningful participation can promote learning communities in which all members' inputs are sought and valued and in which engagement becomes the norm. This can be fostered in different ways:

- View students, parents, and other community members as legitimate and important participants rather than as clients. *Students learn best when they are viewed as workers and when their participation in school affairs is actively solicited because they have legitimate and relevant roles to play.* The school should be a living laboratory in which students practice life skills, such as communication, goal setting, and decision making. *Parents* and other *community members* are more likely to participate when they are viewed as partners with legitimate concerns about and contributions to make to the school's educational process. This does not deny the fact that educators play a centrally important role in the maintenance and development of schools, but schools *belong to the community and are established to serve community-identified needs. They do not belong to educators.*

- Promote the attitude that member participation is important to the school. Everyone has information, suggestions, energy, and skills that can contribute to more effective educational outcomes at the school. In like manner, members need to believe that they are engaged in activities that matter to them. That is, they will feel ownership for what is going on if they value the goals being pursued and they see the potential of positive results, both for themselves and for the community.

- Establish healthy norms for conflict management. Conflicts about ideas are legitimate, but personality attacks are not!

- Offer skill development that prepares members to participate effectively. This includes information and skills focusing on goal setting, teaming, communications, meeting management, consensus decision making, and conflict management.

- Provide sufficient time for participation, and be creative about finding meeting times that are responsive to members' time constraints. The time constraints of all members, not just of educators, need to be taken into consideration.

Record other strategies that can improve meaningful participation in your school:

- _____
  _____
- _____
  _____
- _____
  _____
- _____
  _____

EXERCISE 5.6. Putting the School Roof Back On and Getting Started!

1. In the "Take the Roof Off the School" exercise presented earlier in the chapter (Exercise 5.5), group members were asked to review the six resiliency factors and apply them to the vision of their resilient school of the future. Ask the group to take a few minutes to review the results of that exercise.
2. Next, ask the group to review the strategies suggested for each of the resiliency factors in this section of the chapter. Are any of these strategies worth considering to enhance their school's resiliency-building capacity? Are there others they may want to add? If so, record them next to the results of Exercise 5.5.

Exercise 5.6 provides an opportunity for the group to think about strategies that can enhance the school's resiliency-building capacity.

Schools can change in ways that promote resiliency. We created these organizations, and we have the capacity to re-create them to meet changing needs. In fact, we have the obligation to do so if our assessment indicates that students, educators, and community members are not being well served in ways that promote their long-term resiliency. This chapter has provided a variety of responses to the significant barriers that stand in the way of school resiliency building. We encourage readers to look closely at their own schools, draw relevant conclusions, and make decisions that can improve the resiliency-building capacity of these settings.

> Civilization is a race between education and catastrophe.
>
> —H. G. Wells

The environments we live in significantly affect our resiliency. In Chapter 6, we turn our attention to the environment that surrounds our schools—the communities in which we live and work. Ultimately, the community is the locus in which the long-term ability of our schools to promote student and educator resiliency is determined. If active partnerships of schools and communities are forged, resiliency can be promoted for everyone.

CHAPTER 6

Community Resiliency
Developing Partnerships

Never doubt that small groups of thoughtful, committed citizens can change the world. Indeed, it's the only thing that ever has.

—Margaret Mead

Skepticism that citizens can have a positive influence on their communities marked the last years of the 20th century. We recall a community service announcement on television that created a powerful contrasting image. It began with the silhouette of a person talking about how sure he was that he *could not make a difference* because he *"was just one person."* Another silhouette appeared repeating the same phrase. Within 30 seconds, the television screen was filled with silhouettes lamenting the "fact" that they "could *not* make a difference because [they were] just one person." The message was clear: Yes, each of us is just one person, but *together* we *can* make a difference.

> Even weak men when united are powerful.
> —*Friedrich Schiller*

There are many examples of courageous people who have accomplished extraordinary things. The civil rights movement of the 1960s could never have become a reality without unique individuals, such as Martin Luther King, Jr., Bobby Kennedy, and Rosa Parks who, each in their own way, spoke out about the need for fair treatment and human dignity for everyone. Mahatma Ghandi became the leader of his country because he acted, as an individual, on his beliefs. The countless indi-

> I like the dreams of the future better than the history of the past.
> —*Thomas Jefferson*

viduals who spoke up against the Vietnam War caused our country to move away from a disastrous situation. The citizens of Afghanistan, Czech Republic, Hungary, and Poland rose up to confront the Soviet Union's occupation of their countries and the control of their lives.

> It really takes a community to raise children, no matter how much money one has. Nobody can do it well alone. And it's the bedrock security of community that we and our children need.
> —Marian Wright-Edelman

Similarly, schools and communities are composed of many individuals, most of whom are just ordinary people, but who, together, can do remarkable things. For a community to be healthy and resilient, it takes everyone working together. Unfortunately, many communities and schools do not partner in productive ways. In fact, the opposite may be true. Schools and communities may even view each other as adversaries. Educators and communities can choose to recognize their common destinies and work together to create partnerships for mutual benefit, or they can choose to struggle along in isolation from each other.

The focus of this chapter is on building relationships between schools and their communities. We believe that resilient schools and resilient communities are those that work together as partners. The chapter moves from an exploration of ways to enhance awareness of the need for partnerships between schools and communities to strategies to make this happen. First, we differentiate between communities that exhibit low levels of resiliency and those that exhibit high levels of resiliency. Second, the importance of the community to the successful achievement of the school's role and the importance of the school to the well-being of the community are explored. Last, using the six resiliency factors, strategies for expanding school-community partnerships and making your school and community more resilient are presented.

What Does a Resilient Community Look Like?

Ever since the National Commission on Excellence in Education (1983) report declared that our schools and, by inference, our communities were at risk, we have been debating the validity of this conclusion. This was an important time because of the shift in the public's thinking about schools. For the most part, however, the report and subsequent contributions to the debate have led many of us to beliefs that we need to "fix" individuals who exhibit at-risk behaviors.

Our schools and communities continue to be in trouble, in part at least because of these efforts and the deficit thinking they represent. Goleman (1995) captures the dilemma well:

Over the last decade or so "wars" have been declared, in turn, on teen pregnancy, dropping out, drugs, and most recently, violence. The trouble with such campaigns, though, is that they come too late, after the targeted problem has reached epidemic proportions and taken firm root in the lives of the young. They are crisis interventions, the equivalent of solving a problem by sending an ambulance to the rescue rather than giving an inoculation that would ward off the disease in the first place. (p. 256)

Communities That Need Resiliency Improvement

It is not difficult to find examples of communities that need resiliency improvement. Stories appear daily in newspapers and on TV that remind us of the lack of community resiliency, not only because they are sensational but also because they are so easy to find. For example, we regularly hear about, communities in which young people do not practice protective sex because they believe that they won't live long enough for it to matter, given the profusion of crime and violence that exists in their neighborhoods (McLaughlin, Irby, & Langman, 1994). Similarly, we hear about teenagers who are committing suicide at an alarming rate.

> The game of life is not so much in holding a good hand as playing a poor hand well.
> —H. T. Leslie

A community in need of resiliency can do irreparable damage to the hopes and dreams of those who live in them. Table 6.1 depicts some of the characteristics that typify these communities.

The negative examples illustrated in Table 6.1 are typical of communities that need to grow and become stronger. Are any of these examples representative of your community? Are there others you think should be added to Table 6.1 as it relates to your community?

Communities With Characteristics of Resiliency

We are getting quite good at identifying what does *not* work, but how much do we know about *what does work*? What are the characteristics of a community that exhibits extensive resiliency? In contrast to nonresilient communities, resilient communities tend to exhibit the characteristics listed in Table 6.2. Resilient communities are not likely to be problem free, but they are more likely to confront problems effectively. With all of our efforts to improve the health and well-being of young people and our communities, we still have a long way to go.

> Do what you can with what you have, where you are.
> —Theodore Roosevelt

We each have our own perceptions about the resiliency of the community that we live or work in or both. Exercise 6.1, which follows, can be used in a variety of ways: as a community survey, a

TABLE 6.1 Examples of a Community Needing Resiliency Improvement

Increase Prosocial Bonding	Set Clear and Consistent Boundaries	Teach Life Skills	Provide Caring and Support	Set and Communicate High Expectations	Provide Meaningful Opportunities to Participate
People are isolated	Laws are applied inconsistently	There is denial of problems	Few community services are available	Status quo orientation is maintained	Apathy is evident
Streets are unsafe	Few opportunities exists for community input in governance	Poor problem-identifying and problem-solving skills are apparent	There is need for much greater resources than are made available	A sense of hopelessness prevails	The focus is on differences
A culture of fear and discrimination exists	Tension exists among ethnic, racial, and other groups	There is little evidence of cooperation	Absence of partnerships is the rule	Widespread poor self-esteem or self-concept is apparent	There is minimal infrastructure for citizen input
There is a lack of effective programs	Favoritism is the norm	Ineffective conflict management is common	Individuals feel anonymous	There is little evidence of mutual respect	There is little or no celebration of successes
Little effort to communicate is made	A sense of community is not shared	Teenage pregnancy and other risky behaviors are prevalent	There is an absence of community celebrations	There are few cooperative or cohesive efforts	Few if any community improvement initiatives are undertaken
Lack of trust is common			Leadership is not noticeably visible	There is an absence of community vision	
Factions thrive within the community			Leadership lacks vision		

TABLE 6.2   Examples of a Community With Characteristics of Resiliency

Increase Prosocial Bonding	Set Clear and Consistent Boundaries	Teach Life Skills	Provide Caring and Support	Set and Communicate High Expectations	Provide Meaningful Opportunities to Participate
Citizens engage in meaningful discourse	Norms for participation and decision making are established	Human services collaborations exist	Widespread collaboration on community projects exists	Community supports positive vision for the future	Many civic clubs exist with broad membership
An infrastructure exists that promotes cooperative efforts	Proactivity and acceptance are practiced	Lifelong learning opportunities are available	Respect for law and order is widespread	Quality of life is a high priority	Volunteerism is encouraged
Celebrations and rituals exist	Participatory governance exists	Intergenerational programs are operating	Intergenerational contacts are made	High standards of acceptable behavior are set	Community vision is shared and pursued
Interorganizational activities are common	Emphasis is on community	Preventive programs that are proactive are widespread	Service to others is encouraged	Family and community spirit is prevalent	Leadership training is available and effective
Community symbols are evident	Regular and clear communications exist	Support groups are established		Recognition for efforts and achievements are common	
Meaningful partnerships are nurtured					
Past and current cultures are celebrated					

large group activity, a small group activity, or an individual assessment for each of the stakeholders.

EXERCISE 6.1. Do You Know How Resilient Your Community Is?

1. Duplicate and distribute Tables 6.1 and 6.2 and answer sheet (Handouts 11, 12, and 13 in the Resource section).
2. Ask each person to rate the community's resiliency for each of the six factors. Use the following scale:

   Low Resilience   1   2   3   4   5   High Resilience

3. Develop a group score and identify factors that are low and high in resiliency.
4. List the characteristics that people saw as making the community resilient.
5. List the characteristics that people saw as making the community nonresilient.
6. Agree on priorities that the group may want to discuss further.

Resilient communities not only believe that challenges can be met but that they can grow stronger if they meet them. They are aware of the interdependencies that exist between individuals and families, schools, voluntary organizations, and government agencies. They are aware of the community's problems, they know what its assets are, and they strive for continuous improvement. Genuine participation is invited and listened to seriously. Broad-based support is developed and maintained so that problems can be addressed and, when possible, transformed into assets.

> The world has narrowed into a neighborhood before it has broadened into a brotherhood.
> —Lyndon B. Johnson

Community Assets

We know that the community in which the school operates can make a significant difference in its effectiveness. Recently, there has been documentation of the impact a community can have on its schools and the youth who attend them. One of the leaders in this effort is Peter Benson, president of the Search Institute in Minneapolis, who believes that providing the young with strong foundations during the first two decades of their lives is an important community responsibility (Benson, 1997; Benson et al., 1995). On the basis of data collected across the country, Benson has identified 20 internal and 20 external assets from birth to adulthood (see Handout 15 for a complete list). From these, he extracted 15 characteristics of asset-building communities, which are benchmarks intended to guide community development. As a first review of these characteristics, we think it is more manageable for readers to explore the set of 15 characteristics; Table 6.3 lists them. Benson et al. (1995) conclude that support, boundaries and expectations, empowerment, constructive use of time,

TABLE 6.3 The 15 Characteristics

1. Everyone accepts personal responsibility for building positive personal and relational attitudes and skills, or assets, in youth.
2. The community thinks and acts with everyone, youth and adults, in mind.
3. Values and boundaries for acceptable behaviors are agreed on and modeled by community members.
4. Youth and adults actively reach out to serve others.
5. Families are supported, educated, and encouraged to keep personal and interpersonal asset building a high priority.
6. Youth receive frequent expressed support.
7. Neighborhoods are safe, supportive, and caring.
8. All schools actively promote care, clear and consistent boundaries, and sustained, healthy relationships with adults.
9. Businesses incorporate policies that support family life and embrace asset-building principles for employees.
10. Virtually all 10- to 18-year-olds are involved in one or more groups that hold building personal and community assets as central to their mission.
11. The media (print, radio, television) frequently articulate and support the community's vision and efforts and provide forums to acknowledge and honor the individuals and organizations that have taken innovative actions.
12. All adults who work with youth receive training on how to foster asset building.
13. Youth have opportunities to lead and make decisions.
14. Religious institutions use their resources to foster asset building both within their own programs and in the community.
15. The community exhibits long-term and sustained commitment to asset building.

SOURCE: Adapted from Roehlkepartain and Benson (1996).

educational commitment, positive values, social competencies, and positive identity are eight essential categories to healthy youth development.

To more fully understand the extent to which these assets exist in your community, an assessment must be made. To do this, community members must identify and agree on their community's assets. The intention of Exercise 6.2 is for group members to talk about the core features of a resilient community and the extent to which these core features exist in your community.

In Exercise 6.2, you initiate a conversation about the internal and external assets within your community. The process of identifying needs and strengths, developing a common language, and deciding priorities can build cohesion within the community.

EXERCISE 6.2. Your Community's Assets

This exercise can be used with a school staff, a community group, or both. If the group is large, you may want to divide it into subgroups.

1. To make the task manageable, ask the group to select 3 to 5 of the benchmarks in Table 6.3 (Handout 14 in the Resource section) that are of particular relevance and that can serve as the focus of their work. Ask the group to explore the thinking that led to identifying the assets that were selected.

2. Ask the group to decide where your community currently is regarding each of the assets you have selected, using the following scale:

   Low Resilience   1   2   3   4   5   High Resilience

3. Ask the group to do the same thing concerning where members think it is possible for your community to be in the future for each of these same assets, using the 5-point scale. Then ask group members to discuss their hopes and wishes for the future.

Why Community Support Is Needed for School Resiliency

Partnerships work best when those involved believe they serve their interests. In the past, as far as schools and communities were concerned, this has meant that communities were responsible for supplying students, a plot of land, a building for a school, and funds to pay for operational costs, and educators were responsible for molding the young into contributing community members. However, several events have changed the basic relationship between schools and their communities from one of trust to one of skepticism coupled with a blurring of roles. When more funds began to be generated at the state and federal governmental levels and school district size increased due to natural growth and consolidation, this partnership became more tenuous. Many parents and community members came to the conclusion that they no longer had a say about their schools. Over time, many schools and communities increasingly moved apart. In some instances, they even became adversarial in their relations.

The challenge now is to redefine positive partnering roles for the community in the school and the school in the community. The need is extremely pressing, not only because of the importance of partnering effectively but also because schools are being pressed to do more with fewer resources. When normal sources of support are limited or inadequate, educators seek more resources from their own communities. In fact, this need is driving schools to tap resources and work more collaboratively with their communities. In almost any community, there are extraordinary resource people who are ready and able to provide voluntary services:

- Many senior citizens have the time and interest to work with young people.
- Accomplished individuals want to "give back" by mentoring novices.
- Skilled professionals would like to share their interests with students.

Reform and restructuring efforts have encouraged educators to rethink the ways they operate and why it is so important for them to partner with their communities. In particular, site-based management and decision making have challenged school leaders to collaborate with the community.

Schools that have invited community members to join them in site-based management activities and have used community resources experience the positive results of opening their doors to community participation. Slowly but surely, attitudes begin to change. Schools that thought they were strong only if they maintained some distance from their communities have come to realize that they can do a better job of preparing students when they recognize and act on the need to use all available resources—from the community as well as from within the school.

Why School Support Is Needed for Community Resiliency

Schools have the potential to provide extensive support for the development and maintenance of resilient communities. For example, they can do this in these ways:

> Why should society feel responsible only for the education of children, and not for the education of all adults of every age?
>
> —Erich Fromm

- Preparing the community's youth, through academic and vocational development, to play positive roles as adults
- Encouraging students and staff to engage in service activities that directly support community development
- Being a community focal point by promoting pride and a sense of connectivity through its academic and extracurricular accomplishments
- Being a center for learning for *all* community members
- Developing life skills and leadership skills for parents and other community members

> The man who has ceased to learn ought not to be allowed to wander around loose in these dangerous days.
>
> —M. M. Coady

Fulfilling this potential is quite a formidable task, particularly because many schools and communities tend to apply quick fixes for complex problems. For instance, "Just say no to drugs" may send a clear message, but it does not build the life skills that are necessary to support the intent. Words need to be followed by deeds or little will happen. Untethered drug abuse, crime, and other antisocial behaviors that contribute to the schools' problems require communitywide responses.

From Reactive to Proactive Community Relationships

The important thing is to recognize that schools *can* partner with their communities. For this to become a reality, reforms and resources may be required, but with will power, it can happen. In fact, Chapter 8 provides information about many communities around the country where it *is* happening.

What do mutually beneficial partnerships between schools and their communities look like? To visualize such partnerships, we summarize how schools and communities have typically interacted in the past and identify the trends that are currently evolving toward more positive and effective partnerships in the future. Table 6.4 graphically displays a reactive-to-proactive school and community relationships scale.

> That which seems the height of absurdity in one generation often becomes the height of wisdom in another.
>
> —*Adlai Stevenson*

Table 6.4 illustrates five types of relationships, varying from those that typified school-community interactions of the past, *closed systems* and *tolerance,* to those that we believe are and will typify school-community interactions of the future, *connectivity* and *outreach. Community involvement* is the middle point of the continuum.

Closed Systems

Schools on the reactive end of the continuum are *closed systems.* They minimize contacts, which are viewed as being bothersome and intrusive. Parents and other community members are seen as adversaries rather than partners, critics rather than supporters, and incapable of making meaningful inputs rather than being relevant and equal voices at the table. They believe that the important task of educating youngsters should be left to those qualified to do this—educators. In short, parents and community members should assist schools only when they are asked to do so.

Tolerance

To the extent that these closed schools find themselves pressed to interact, they relate with *tolerance.* They posture about involvement but keep control of the process. For example, many school Parent-Teachers Associations

(PTAs) or Parent-Teachers Organizations (PTOs) send signals that only a select group of parents are valued and that educators will provide the leadership and be the dominant force. Schools using the tolerance approach may request parental involvement but typically only when academic or disciplinary problems regarding their children arise. Educators who function this way provide only the information they want community members to know and do so in ways that limit feedback and discussion.

> When an individual is kept in a situation of inferiority, the fact is that he does become inferior.
> —Simone de Beauvior

In the past, most community members believed this was the way it should be, but not many do today. As tasks associated with schooling become more complex and more controversial, parents and other community members are less willing to acquiesce to educators. Instead, they are demanding a more direct role in the process for themselves.

> In the end, education must be education toward the ability to decide.
> —Victor Frankl

When there is apathy or adversarial relations between the school and the community, the cost is tremendous: Community support and development are diminished, defensive and isolated schools proliferate, and special interest groups detract from support for the welfare of the larger community.

Community Involvement

More energies are going into the development of mutually beneficial relations between schools and their communities. Reactive systems are outdated, as is the expectation that meaningful education can occur without engaging the energies and participation of community members. The African proverb "It takes a village to raise a child" has never been more true, especially given the increasingly complex nature of the task. The trouble is, our villages are becoming more difficult to define because they are growing larger, the boundaries between them are becoming blurred, and traditional institutions, such as the church and the home, seem to be less willing or able to play their parts in keeping the village together.

This vacuum has led to experimentation with different configurations in which there is purposeful nurturing of community involvement on the part of schools. The past two decades have witnessed an increasing number of efforts that encourage communities to bring their resources to bear on improved service for children. Furthermore, schools are becoming one-stop shopping centers for parents seeking child-related services. For example, welfare and mental health agencies are being invited to set up shop in many schools. The intent is that, working cooperatively in a single setting, these agencies, in partnership with schools, can better coordinate services to meet the needs of children.

There are also increasing efforts to enlist community resource people. Examples of these resource people are senior citizens who have the time

TABLE 6.4 School and Community: From Reactive to Proactive Relations

	Closed	Tolerant	Involved	Connected	Outreaching
Beliefs	• Locked down mentality	• Grudging acceptance of legitimate, but limited, role of parents in school	• Community support for school sought and encouraged	• Active networking to develop communitywide, comprehensive, integrated programs	• Mutual support and partnerships
Expectations	• Minimal involvement of parents (controlled by school staff) • Limited time set aside for engagement	• Limited and formalized engagement in school affairs for parents and possibly others in community	• Parents and others actively involved • Social agencies encouraged to collaborate on youth-related activities	• Extensive open, flexible and ongoing relationship between community and school	• All community elements represented • Equal access for initiation, involvement, and decision making
Governance structures	• Explicit and detailed policies or rules for parent involvement set by the school	• Advice sought from select group of parents (PTA or PTO) • School-dominated governance and decision making • PTAs or PTOs dominated by educators	• School sets parameters but seeks active involvement with parents and community	• Schools and other agencies focus on youth and meet together regularly to set priorities and monitor activities	• Interagency councils • Nonbureaucratic and fluid structures that promote mutual influence

Communications	• Highly limited and one-way, from school to parents	• Primarily one-way, from school to parents and community	• School-initiated feedback encouraged from parents and community • Invitational and regular to parents and community	• Two-way and formalized with youth-related agencies and other organizations	• Multichanneled • Two-way • Frequent
Resources	• Minimal resources set aside for relationship purposes • Parents or community resources not pursued	• PTA/PTO fund raising for school priorities • Room Mothers or Fathers with limited roles • Focus limited to students and classroom needs	• Resources for the school identified and solicited	• School facilities made available for community use • Community facilities made available for school use	• School personnel and students engaged as community volunteers
Activities	• School calls on parents when student-related problems arise • Formal and limited parent committees	• Structured and limited parent committees • Principal apprises parents and others of school activities	• Students mentored by community members • Volunteers sought for school programs • Social service agencies function in the school	• Shared use of facilities (e.g., meeting rooms, libraries, and computers) • Summer programs developed cooperatively to meet community needs	• Agreed-on joint initiatives that focus on community improvement • Service learning

and interest to work with children, mentors who provide positive role modeling by spending quality time with one or two students, tutors who work with children on a one-to-one basis, and individuals who share special talents and life experiences with young people.

Last, efforts that emphasize that schools are here to serve communities are becoming more prevalent. For instance, open houses, coffee hours for realtors, bicycle roundups, and community day celebrations are just a few of the ways this effort to serve is being expressed.

Connectivity

As community involvement successes expand, a new level of proactive relations between schools and communities, *connectivity*, is spreading. Connective relations are those in which schools and other youth-related agencies cooperate and coordinate to develop comprehensive communitywide programs for youth and adults. Connectivity means opening schools for mutually beneficial program endeavors. These include summer programs for youth and other community members, adult learner initiatives, and making school facilities available for community uses and community facilities available for school uses.

Outreach

Moving to the cutting edge of the continuum, *outreach* efforts are being initiated by schools that purposefully try to have a direct and positive impact on the community. These are schools that promote service learning, encourage staff and students to participate in community improvement efforts, and take initiatives to bring diverse agencies and volunteer organizations together for mutual understanding, problem solving, and comprehensive improvement efforts. Such schools recognize that they and their communities have much to gain by working together and helping each other. Joint interest is evident, efforts are cooperative, and successes are mutually celebrated.

> People should think things out fresh and not just accept conventional terms and the conventional way of doing things.
> —Buckminster Fuller

We are most likely to do those things for which we will be rewarded. Educators are not usually rewarded for reaching out to the community. Most school districts do not support educator outreach and connectivity to the community. As important, community leaders do not often see the relevance of working with educational leaders to see how they can be of mutual assistance. These dynamics can change, but it will take individuals and groups who have the courage to think and act differently and who are willing to develop shared, cooperative plans and strategies to improve everyone's resiliency.

> You have not done enough, you have never done enough, so long as it is still possible that you have something to contribute.
> —Dag Hammarskjöld

It is a long way from the reactive closed school to the proactive outreach school, because it means changing beliefs as well as behaviors. The journey will have to be taken one step at a time. It may take considerable time and effort to make the shift from one end of the continuum to the other, but it is important to take the journey if we are to meet the challenges faced by schools and communities. The purpose of Exercise 6.3 is to help your group assess where your school and community currently are on the reactive-proactive scale and identify what may be needed to move your school and community closer to the proactive end of the scale.

We hope this exercise will help those who participated to be clearer about the ways the school and the community related in the past, how they relate now, and how they would prefer them to relate in the future.

EXERCISE 6.3. Making Proactivity a Part of Your Day

1. Distribute copies of Table 6.4: Schools and Communities: From Reactive to Proactive Relations (Handout 16 in the Resource section). Ask members to review it and determine which column most closely represents the current situation in your community. Ask the group to come to a consensus about the closest fit for your school and community.
2. Ask the group to explore why the current situation exists. What have the schools done that have led to it? What has the community done that has led to it? Ask someone to write agreements for each question on chart paper or on a chalkboard.
3. Where the group views relationships between the school and the community as being reactive, what changes may be needed to move away from this direction? What resources will be needed? List changes and resources needed on chart paper or the chalkboard.
4. Where the group categorizes the school and community relationship as being proactive, what do you think it will take to remain at this level or, better yet, become even more proactive? List strategies and resources.

Strategies for Improving Community Resiliency

The road to health and strength is strewn with difficulties for many troubled communities, especially if willing hands to help are limited and problems are extensive. The fewer the number of people committed to working on resiliency-promoting activities, the more the likelihood that gangs, drugs, and violence will be widespread. Even when positive efforts are pursued, most are likely to be isolated projects rather than comprehensive efforts that promote networking and connectivity across the larger community. Even when agencies receive funds for cross-agency projects, there is still no guarantee that they will be systematically coordinated or that they will involve representatives from schools or the community.

To help readers who want to implement resiliency-building strategies in their communities, we return to the factors on the Resiliency Wheel (see Figure 1.2). The discussion of the barriers and strategies for each of the six factors is intended to stimulate thinking about the situation in your community and how best to improve it. Readers are encouraged to modify suggested strategies and add others that might be helpful in making your community more resilient.

Increase Prosocial Bonding

This factor is difficult to address. Too frequently, community members have limited knowledge about each other, given the high mobility rate that exists in so many communities. Compounding the situation, schools may not even reflect their communities because reform and desegregation initiatives shuffle students to and from schools and even across school districts. This disconnectiveness is compounded by the double-edged sword of technology. Instant communication can be life saving, opening worlds to people and connecting them quickly. But it can also reduce or be a substitute for face-to-face involvement and hinder community bonding.

Strategies for Increasing Prosocial Bonding

Caring adults exist in every community. The challenge is to find ways of expanding the core group of highly active adults by tapping into others who have not yet become involved. Communities that can tap into these latent resources are more likely to become healthier and stronger.

Bonding occurs when people connect with each other. There are many untapped resources in almost any community that can increase connectivity. Here are some strategies to consider:

- Connect young people with individuals who are positive role models. They can be found in organizations such as Big Sisters and Big Brothers and PTOs and PTAs. Or they may just be individuals in the community who are able and willing to be mentors. Thinking of such connections as expanding the circle of friends may help stimulate similar connectivity initiatives.

> The family you come from isn't as important as the family you're going to have.
>
> —*Ring Lardner*

- Identify resource people in your community. For example, retired persons are excellent resources. They can be invited to help in the school, work in the library, be mentors for students, and give demonstrations regarding subjects they know about.

- Create opportunities for communities and schools to bond by reaching out to help each other—for example, by extending community access to school facilities and putting on school-community fairs.

- Promote multiage and intergenerational connectivity through rewarding activities. For example, all-night basketball courts in urban centers can bring people of all ages together to meet and talk while shooting hoops. Similarly, continuing education opportunities can bring people from across the community to learn together.

- Bring community members together in settings that promote positive discussion about important issues and initiatives. Town-hall-type meetings can involve leaders from the local government, schools, higher education institutions, and business and voluntary organizations, as well as other citizens.

- Provide a directory of organizations that support the community's mission and goals. This low-cost activity can be quite important. It communicates what resources there are in the community and lets people know how to access them.

Record other strategies that can increase prosocial bonding for your community:

- _____
  _____
- _____
  _____
- _____
  _____

Set Clear and Consistent Boundaries

The larger the community, the more likely it is to exhibit diversity, which can be a powerful community-building asset. The diversity of cultures, values, and traditions within the community can be a rich resource but only if it can be tapped effectively. The more diverse the community, the more boundaries are needed to clarify behavioral expectations. Many communities either do not have adequate boundary-related structures in place to address community issues or else these structures are not used effectively. To further complicate matters, many expectations for behaviors may be unwritten, unclear, or even contradictory.

Strategies for Promoting Clear and Consistent Boundaries

Communities can define boundaries that help citizens interact safely and effectively with each other. For this to happen, all voices need to be represented when laws, policies, rules, norms, and other expectations are discussed and agreed on because involvement creates ownership and understanding. Strategies to promote effective and agreed-on boundaries include:

- View rules as a way of taking care of each other and as a way of promoting opportunities for growth and development, not as a way of disciplining people. Families need to set rules and consequences to promote positive relationships; neighbors need to take responsibility for monitoring youth behaviors; schools need to establish clear rules and consequences, positive and negative, for both young people and the adults who work with them; and communities need to set rules that promote acceptable behavior—for instance, at gatherings and when driving.

- Promote community involvement in clarifying and resolving school-based issues. For example, one school in a high crime area had a persistent problem with teachers' cars being broken into or stolen. With the involvement of neighborhood families whose homes bordered the school, the thefts stopped. Neighbors called the police when they saw what was happening and, more effectively, they got the word out in the community for it to stop. In a very short time, it did!

- Conduct town hall meetings that can be used to set norms and expectations for the community. But be sure to identify the best time for the majority of the community to meet. Do not assume that an evening meeting time is best for everyone.

Record other strategies that can promote clear and consistent boundaries for all members of your community:

- _____
  _____
- _____
  _____
- _____
  _____

Teach Life Skills

Navigating the waters of society can be treacherous without the ability to communicate effectively, make decisions, and manage conflict. These skills, along with having a sense of purpose, are particularly needed in large, complex, and diverse communities. It is not realistic to expect effective participation if community members do not possess necessary skills or when some members, such as government and school leaders, have them and others do not. Such disparities often lead to conflict and distrust.

Strategies for Fostering Life Skills

The well-being of the community is highly dependent on the ability of its members to interact with each other effectively, particularly in efforts to improve the community's resiliency-building capacity. In turn, the ability to interact effectively is based on skill development. Strategies to bring this about include:

- Train community leaders, both youth and adults, in key skill areas. For example, the National Parent-Teacher Association offers a comprehensive program for parents who want to learn to be better leaders. Such programs are most helpful if they are based on a "training of trainers" model, wherein participants learn skills and then help others learn them.

- Identify resource people within the community who have particular skills and experiences that can be of help to others. For example, community volunteers can help youngsters develop life skills through career day programs. Community organizations can encourage interested members to help various segments of the community. Cross-organizational planning and coordination of needed services can enhance efficiency and effectiveness. Most important, equitability of services should be promoted so that those who need them the most receive them.

- Teach assessment techniques to clarify life skill needs so the community can identify both strengths and challenges and make good decisions about uses of its resources.

- Provide life skill learning opportunities through continuing education.

Record other strategies that can foster life skills for all community members:

- _____
  _____
- _____
  _____
- _____
  _____

Provide Caring and Support

Too many communities are isolating places, places where people stay apart and may even fear each other. Communities that provide caring and support for young people, the elderly, and those in between develop strong connections that can help individuals, families, schools, and neighborhoods through hard times. If care and support are practiced in the home, the neighborhood, the school, and the community, people will feel that they matter.

Strategies for Enhancing Caring and Support

Caring and support are sustained through connections and a sense of belonging. Some strategies to promote care and support include the following:

- Identify caring members in the community who can be on call to provide support to people, from young children to senior citizens, who may need help. This group can be expanded over time as others come forward and make the commitment to volunteer.

- Place high value on caring. This can be promoted through formal campaigns (e.g., billboards and radio and television announcements) and informal means, such as good role modeling by leaders. Learning to care about others is what makes the difference in building connectivity and community. This is true whether referring to students and staff in schools or adults and children in families, neighborhoods, and communities.

- Provide recognition for positive behaviors. Catching people doing things right ought to be the bias, rather than catching them doing things wrong. For example, efforts of students and community members who take care of themselves and take the time to care for others can be publicized and celebrated.

- Work with the media to get stories that demonstrate caring and support out to the public. For this to happen, relationships with the media must be nurtured and developed over time, not just when a favorable story needs to be broadcast: Invite the media to cover important school and community stories, respond quickly when they call for information, and be empathetic to their constraints—they have deadlines that you can help them meet.

Record other strategies that can enhance caring and support for community members:

- _____
  _____
- _____
  _____

Set and Communicate High Expectations

What a difference the words we use and the attitudes we have can make. Saying "we can" and "we will" instead of "we can't" and "we won't" or saying "when we . . ." instead of "if we . . ." can create hope and motivation instead of fatalism and minimal efforts. Putting the emphasis on "we" rather than "you" sends a powerful message. Whereas some communities tend to use positive, encompassing, and inviting language, others tend to use negative and divisive language. The language that is communicated is extraordinarily important.

> Nothing splendid has ever been achieved except by those who dared believe that something inside them was superior to circumstances.
> —*Bruce Barton*

Regardless of sociodemographics or other unique factors, neighborhoods need to believe in themselves, be supported by others, and join together to form viable communities. Reaching out to build belief in capabilities within and across neighborhoods sets a tone for the growth and development of communities. Schools and neighborhoods also need to reach out and see each other as mutual supporters rather than concluding that they are left on their own to cope with issues. Besides promoting distrust and alienation, isolation removes people from direct responsibility and reduces the pressure to achieve, let alone excel.

Strategies for Strengthening High Expectations

Changing attitudes is the starting place. Before action can take place as a community, members need to share beliefs that the community can become what its members want it to be. Improvement needs to be viewed as a necessity, not an option. Most of all, promoting high expectations for a community means promoting dialogue—community members cannot remain silent, accepting the ways things are, and still expect great things to happen. Changing the "can'ts" to "cans," the "wants" to "wills," and the "ifs" to "whens" requires the following kinds of strategies:

> Improvement is a necessity, not an option.
> —*Bill Blokker*

- Promote service. Students can be engaged in service learning, but adults can also be challenged to volunteer their time, skills, and talents. Service-oriented communities are those in which all age groups help others achieve in meaningful ways. Youth, adults, and senior citizens can all give in ways that improve the community.

- Create rituals and celebrations that honor efforts and achievements of individuals, groups, schools, voluntary organizations, neighborhoods, and the local government. Community celebrations are important because they send the message that there is pride in members' achievements. It also reminds members about what they hold in common and that the community resiliency vision is being pursued.

- Work with the media to publicize progress and positive outcomes by individuals, groups, neighborhoods, schools, and the entire community. There are few things more exciting than witnessing the transformation of a community. Making it happen is the major task, of course, but telling the story is also important. Sharing positive results builds ownership and spreads participation. Besides, it reflects the resiliency message, turning the focus from finding the negative to finding the positive. This culture-modifying activity is a difficult task, but it can happen if everyone involved focuses on getting the message across and supports each other's efforts.

- Identify and promote projects that are meaningful and challenge community members. Changing communities means moving into unknown territory and taking risks.

- Encourage everyone, adults as well as the young, to try their best and to succeed. All of us—educators, parents, and community members—need to participate, point the way, show confidence, and commit to supporting efforts. "You can do it and I'm going to help you in any way I can" is a powerful resiliency-building message.

Record other strategies that can strengthen high expectations for community members:

- _____
  _____
- _____
  _____
- _____
  _____

Provide Opportunities for Meaningful Participation

Community problem solving, decision making, and goal setting are activities that are often restricted to those who are in formal leadership positions and those connected to them in some influential way. Even when community meetings are held, too often core issues are not addressed, input is not sought, and decisions are already made. These showcase meetings leave us with the feeling that our time is being wasted. If our experiences are negative, we are likely to withdraw. We may even become opponents of the direction that is being taken.

Even when wider and more genuine participation is sought, it is difficult for community members to find the time to engage in the conversation. Time for dialogue is a critically important resource for meaningful participation. Unfortunately, it is in short supply for both educators and community members. As educators focus on content delivery and engage in school improvement efforts, less quality time seems to be available to connect with the community. For their part, most community members work and do not have the opportunity to meet with educators during the daytime when schools are in session. This is a bigger problem today than ever before, in part because of increasing numbers of households with single working parents and in part because even where there are two parents, in many instances both are likely to be working and unavailable to interact with each other, let alone with educators. Some educators are taking the initiative to meet at business locations instead of requiring everyone to come to the school.

Strategies for Improving Meaningful Participation

Reaching out to involve community members can seem like an overwhelming task because there are so many people to be engaged and so many voices to be heard. However, the payoff of working together can make a meaningful difference. Some useful strategies include the following:

> We are not going to be able to operate our spaceship earth successfully nor for much longer unless we see it as a whole spaceship and our fate as common. It has to be everybody or nobody.
> —Buckminster Fuller

- Hold a series of town-hall-type meetings, bringing representatives of all segments of the community together to create a vision, priorities, goals, and expectations for positive contributions by community members. The process is just as important as the product; it promotes networking and support. Furthermore, summarizing and disseminating the results spreads the word, making the meaning more tangible and providing the basis for further discussions and planning for ongoing improvement.

- Invite the media's involvement. The media can get the message out to people and provide a forum for the exchange of views. They can also write editorials. But for all of this to happen, they need to become active partners.

- Develop responses to people's inability to be involved. For example, people with children who would like to participate can be provided with child care, not only to increase their involvement but also to model a service-learning community approach. Community members who do not have access to transportation can be brought into the dialogue and car-pooling arrangements developed. Even simply holding meetings at alternative times and at more convenient locations can make a big difference for busy citizens.

- Develop ways of connecting that emphasize the personal touch—for example, by including different community voices and perspectives during planning and being knowledgeable about cultural differences and honoring them by provid-

> The good neighbor looks beyond the external accidents and discerns those inner qualities that make all men human, and, therefore, brothers.
> —Martin Luther King, Jr.

ing translators when some community members are non-English speakers. Tap into local organizations that have experiences with diversity to provide needed assistance and establish a Web site for information and dialogue to be shared.

- Get beyond conversation to make plans and take specific actions. Community members are more likely to continue to participate if they believe that something will come of all the talk and suggestions. Attending to the priorities that are set so that outcomes are generated is just as important as getting the process started. For example, if a weekly coffee klatch is instituted to talk about community issues and a list of ideas is generated, it is important that progress reports are made at future gatherings. These reports should include descriptions of any plans and activities that have been initiated. This kind of feedback fuels momentum and builds interest and enthusiasm.

- Develop a common language system that defines terms related to healthy, resilient communities. Shared meaning is a critical foundation. We need to understand each other before we can come together to support shared purposes. This can be promoted by creating teams of school and community-based volunteers to carry the message to the rest of the community. In fact, such a team approach models the process for building community resiliency while it provides opportunities for people to become conversant with the basic elements of resilient communities.

Record other suggestions for improving opportunities for meaningful participation:

- _____
  _____
- _____
  _____
- _____
  _____

Community resiliency building is a challenging task that requires broad-based commitment and support. It also requires the willingness to admit shortcomings as well as the desire to publicize strengths. Getting started means making a realistic appraisal of where things are *now*. Table 6.5 is intended to be a map to help the community engage in this important task.

Exercise 6.4 focuses on the priorities needed to increase your community's resiliency. It can move participants a step closer to agreement about resiliency-building strategies to apply in the community.

Nothing in life is to be feared. It is only to be understood.
—*Marie Curie*

TABLE 6.5 Building Resiliency in Our Community: Now and Tomorrow

	Increase Prosocial Bonding	*Set Clear and Consistent Boundaries*	*Teach Life Skills*	*Provide Caring and Support*	*Communicate High Expectations*	*Provide Meaningful Participation*
Community as it currently exists						
Community of the future						

EXERCISE 6.4. Moving a Step Closer to a Resilient Community

It will be helpful if a cross section of community members is involved in the activity, which is best done in groups of 6 to 8 people. Ensure that everyone has a copy of Table 6.5 (Handout 17 in the Resource section).

1. Ask group members to identify resiliency-building activities that are *presently* going on in the community. Have them list things they agree about in the "Now" row of their copy of the handout.
2. What are the community's greatest strengths? How did these things evolve? Does the discussion provide any insights for future resiliency-building initiatives?
3. Review the strategies presented in the chapter. Are any of these relevant for your community? Ask members to write things they agree about pursuing in the "Tomorrow" row.
4. Ask the group to review and prioritize the strategies on which it would like to focus your community's energies and resources. How can these priorities be put in place?

Communities can work together to become stronger, healthier, and more resilient. Different voices can be like chimes in the wind, blending together to make a beautiful melody. This chapter has built on the foundation created in the previous chapters to suggest ways of harmonizing these voices, including those of students, educators, and other members of the community. Chapter 7 focuses on two processes that are necessary if this is going to happen—facilitation of the process and assessment of progress, including the current status and potential for community resiliency building, monitoring activities, and establishing results.

PART III

Making It Happen for Schools & Communities

Facilitating Resiliency Development

Strategies for Managing and Assessing Change

Even if you're on the right track, you'll get run over if you just sit there.
—Will Rogers

Bringing It All Together and Facilitating Resiliency Development

Part I focused on the concepts of resiliency and community. Part II delved into specifics about building resiliency for students, educators, organizations, and communities. In both parts, exercises were suggested to help readers gain a clearer understanding of how schools and communities grow healthier. Part III suggests ways of bringing it all together. This chapter concentrates on two vitally important areas: implementing resiliency strategies and determining the effectiveness of the change effort. In Chapter 8, examples of efforts to build resilient schools and communities are highlighted.

Understanding resiliency concepts is the foundation for building a resilient community. The next step is to implement the concepts. To help

AUTHORS' NOTE: There are no exercises in Chapters 7 and 8 because the emphasis shifts from *understanding* to *implementing* resiliency.

readers implement resiliency strategies, five areas are highlighted: (a) stages of change, (b) group development, (c) leadership needs, (d) facilitation skills, and (e) assessment and evaluation of progress. Strategies are suggested to improve chances of successful implementation of resiliency initiatives.

Stages of Change

Understanding the stages of change is critical to efforts to build resilient communities. It is easy to get stuck if people who are leading the efforts do not recognize and proceed with courage through the stages of change: initiation, implementation, institutionalization, and refocusing (Fullan, 1991, 1993; Hord, Rutherford, Huling-Austin, & Hall, 1987).

> Trust yourself in the deep, uncharted waters. When there is a storm it is safer in the open sea. If you stay too near the dock you will get beaten to death.
>
> —Sam Keen

Initiation

The *initiation* stage focuses on personal concerns and readiness to become engaged in the effort. Building awareness, providing information, making resources available, developing relevance, and a capacity for planning are key considerations at this stage. People will want to know why it is important to build resiliency and how it will affect them. Many of their questions will center on costs and benefits for themselves.

> A man convinced against his will is not convinced.
>
> —Laurence J. Peter

At the outset only a small group of people will probably be ready to move forward, whereas others will need to be helped to join the effort and to move through each stage at their own comfort level. Leaders need to reflect on these differences if they hope to build ownership and trust. Information needs to be provided to address personal concerns so resources and people can be mobilized toward implementation. Miles's (1987) review of major research studies found "that a combination of strong advocacy, need, active initiation, and a clear model for proceeding characterized . . . successful startups" (p. 62).

Strategies to Consider During the Initiation Stage

- Develop a critical mass of people who are supportive and willing to take active roles in implementing plans to build resiliency throughout the community. This can be facilitated by meeting with key people in the school district and the community to discuss building a resilient community, conducting town-hall-type meetings for the purposes of learning about resiliency and the impact it can have on the community, and by initiating planning activities. Be sure to include representatives from the different segments of the community in these deliberations.

- Recruit people who can, in turn, bring others on board.

- Help participants understand that change is likely to be a long process.

- Check for signs of readiness—does it appear that there are more supporters than detractors?

Implementation

Implementation, the next stage of change, "consists of the process of putting into practice an idea, program, or set of activities and structures new to the people attempting or expected to change" (Fullan, 1991, p. 65).

During this stage, people should be more concerned about getting tasks completed than about their personal issues. Because it is a new experience for most people and mistakes are likely to be made, the intensity of involvement will probably be heightened, conflicts will arise, and planning time may be resisted in favor of taking action. Uneasiness may set in if members feel that they are involved with uncertainty—something akin to building a rocket while it is flying. This uneasiness must be managed effectively. Fullan (1985) says that effective approaches have combining and balancing factors that do not apparently go together—simultaneous simplicity-complexity, looseness-tightness, strong leadership-participation (or simultaneous bottom up-top downness), fidelity-adaptivity, and evaluation-nonevaluation. More than anything else, effective strategies for improvement require an understanding of the process, a way of thinking (p. 399).

> Change means movement, movement means friction, friction means heat, and heat means controversy. The only place where there is no friction is in outer space or a seminar on political action.
>
> —Saul Alinsky

Strategies to Consider During the Implementation Stage

- Provide safety nets so that "mistakes" can be viewed as part of the learning process.

- Focus on visioning questions, such as "What will be different when our community becomes more resilient?"

- Identify the key players in the change process (e.g., educational leaders, local government officials, leaders of higher education institutions, leaders of voluntary organizations, other key leaders, and other community members) and connect them with each other so they do not have to act in isolation.

- Provide "early rewards and some tangible success are critical incentives during implementation" (Fullan, 1991, p. 69). Reinforcement of new behaviors is a powerful force, so it is important to identify and celebrate successes and provide rewards.

Institutionalization

Much time and effort will probably be spent on the start up and implementation of plans to build a more resilient community. The next stage, *institutionalization*, occurs when the initiative moves from an innovation to become an integral part of the structure. This is the point in time when many initiatives are discontinued because it takes continued focus and much time (Berman & McLaughlin, 1978; Fullan, 1991; Huberman & Miles, 1984; Schorr, 1998). Few survive to become part of the fabric.

> I was taught that the way of progress is neither swift nor easy.
>
> —Marie Curie

Strategies to Consider During the Institutionalization Phase

- Foster collaboration so that resiliency becomes central to members' daily lives. Supporting and connecting people who want to collaborate sustains the level of engagement.

- Secure resources. Whereas resources are not particularly unique to this phase, they are quite important because decisions to continue or cut funding affects institutionalization.

- Involve stakeholders from the community through different activities. Check to see if people are involved and invite those who are not. Then, monitor interactions to be sure that group development is ongoing.

- Build resiliency plans as well as structures, budgets, policies, procedures, and support to make the plans come to life.

- Help people see the links between continuing resiliency-building efforts and community improvements.

Refocusing

Refocusing, the last stage, emphasizes two areas: process improvements and outcomes. Like the old saying, "The storm comes before the rainbow appears," at this stage, the community will have weathered many storms and have grown through challenges and opportunities. People will have grappled with the meaning of change and learned new skills. It is now time to reflect on the journey, improve performance, and celebrate outcomes.

> Start with what they know.
> Build with what they have.
> —*Lao Tsu*

In the initiation stage, the journey began because some people believed that the community could be healthier and stronger. Now, at the refocusing stage, new behaviors need to be reinforced to sustain these beliefs. In addition, a foundation for ownership needs to be fostered by including different stakeholders, providing relevant information, and encouraging ever-broader bands of community members to participate in their own ways and at their own paces.

The refocusing stage is the time to confirm outcomes and consider ways of improving them. At this stage of change, people should have a sense of pride, feel good about what they are doing, and be ready to focus on refining and further developing resiliency initiatives.

A few cautions are in order. First, change is not a linear process. More than likely, some individuals will just be entering the initiation stage while others are already at the implementation or refocusing stage. Care should be given to plan for people being able to enter the process at different times. Second, significant change does not occur rapidly. Members need to understand that most goals will not be realized during the first year. In reality, it may take 3 to 5 years, or more, for the process to become institutionalized. Last, many of our initial assumptions may not hold true. For example, in all probability,

- Although a plan is needed to make change happen, the process will change from how you planned it.

- There will be disagreements and conflict.

- People will change their positions and beliefs, sometimes in ways that are not predictable.

- Despite great efforts, not everyone will change.

- There will be multiple reasons why change may not be embraced, including lack of resources, time, skills, and understanding.

Group Development

Understanding the stages of change is critical to efforts to build resilient communities, but it is also important to be aware that community resiliency development is conducted in groups that must work together effectively. Groups that work cooperatively for common causes are relatively unique. They need to be nurtured and supported or they will be in constant turmoil.

> Few, if any, forces in human affairs are as powerful as a shared vision.
> —*Peter Senge*

It is great fun to be a part of a group that is energetic and productive. If people within a group have similar values and beliefs and have compatible work ethics and skills, the group will probably function at a productive level. If they don't, it can result in chaos and, more important, jeopardize resiliency initiatives.

Phases of group development parallel the stages of change. But whereas the stages of change focus on the overall plan, group development is about building capacity through relationships. According to Tuckman (1965), there are five phases of group growth: *forming, storming, norming, performing,* and *disbanding.* Positive group development takes careful orchestration during each of these phases.

The first phase, *forming,* is when people get to know each other as they join together to achieve common purposes. They have not yet become a team. They are not focused on tasks, they wait and watch until they know what their roles will be. Issues have to do with encouraging involvement and cohesion.

> Working with people is difficult, but not impossible.
> —Peter Drucker

The second phase, *storming,* is characterized by conflict—vying for power, leadership rights and behaviors, and control issues within the group—as members begin to address these hard issues. If members learn conflict management skills, this phase may be easier to process. But if leaders try to control all conflicts, the group will not have the chance to develop and sort out the issues.

The third phase, *norming,* focuses on establishing norms, procedures, and policies. Group members explore roles and learn how to work through conflicts. Structure is established so that people can work together without constant storming. Acceptable norms of behavior are agreed on, including establishing expectations for meetings, such as starting on time, preparing and being ready to participate effectively, and following established procedures. An identity as a group is formed as expectations for group behavior and sanctions for group members who fail to meet these expectations are developed.

The fourth phase, *performing,* emerges as conflicts are resolved and structures are established. At this stage, group members work together well—everyone is actively involved, accomplishing tasks and objectives and supporting norms and structures. At this stage, the group should be focused on performance and outcomes.

Not all groups reach the performing phase. In fact, some never get past forming! Outside assistance may be required to help groups work through issues and move on to the next phase of development, and group skills may need to be developed before members can work together effectively. Furthermore, as new members join the group, time must be allotted to help them move through the four phases. Effective groups take time to help new members through the stages. It is better to do this up front than later when problems may arise.

Last, groups need to *disband* when tasks are completed. Members need to be released so that they can focus on other ongoing activities and emerging tasks. Human resources are at a premium, especially for voluntary initiatives, such as community resiliency building.

Groups can become productive, grow, develop interdependence, and collaborate effectively. But it takes time to create such groups. In this regard, it might be useful for group members to reflect on the story, *The Sense of a Goose* (Handout 18 in the Resource section). When working with groups, we have to help each other make the journey by sharing leadership, being empathetic when others have problems, and supporting each other through the process.

Leadership Needs

Leadership, especially within voluntary, self-managed teams, is extremely important. Leadership can ensure that members share authority and responsibility and that work is coordinated. Self-managed teams need leadership to establish "clearly defined objectives, appropriate task design, appropriate size and membership, substantial authority and discretion, an adequate information system, appropriate recognition and rewards, strong support, adequate interpersonal skills, and appropriate socialization of members" (Yukl, 1998, p. 363). In addition, diversity must be appreciated and nurtured by group leaders.

> Like effective parents, lovers, teachers, and therapists, good leaders make people helpful.
> —*Warren Bennis*

Leadership can have a major effect on the building of resiliency. How leadership evolves and functions will play a significant role in who participates, how effectively they participate, how teams are managed, how people are motivated, and whether they will be empowered during the process. Here are some key leadership functions that need to be considered:

Key stakeholders, including those who are critical of the effort, should be recruited and involved. Selecting only people who will be supportive, or at least will not be resistors, can create a false sense of effectiveness. Just as we need challenges to become more resilient, so do we need challenges to implement solid, well-thought-out plans and actions. Knowing who the critics are and why they can be expected to resist is as important as knowing who the supporters of the change are. No one person or elite group of people can create a vision and plan for diverse communities. All key stakeholders need to be involved.

People will be motivated if goals and activities are relevant to them. The vision has to communicate clearly and meaningfully; resiliency building is needed not just for some but for

> The salvation of mankind lies only in making everything the concern for all.
> —*Alexander I. Solzhenitsyn*

everyone. Creating a sense of urgency about the need for change promotes the development of a learning community that can support and nurture the process and product. In short, "build a broad coalition to support the change" (Yukl, 1998, p. 449).

"People learn new patterns of behavior primarily through their interactions with others, not through front-end training designs" (Fullan, 1993, p. 68). This means that ongoing involvement and positive relationships need to be fostered.

People must be prepared for the realities of change. They must know that change is like a roller coaster ride; there will be highs and lows, progress and setbacks. It is important to help people understand the process by letting them know about the problems that are likely to crop up. This can ease the trauma of change.

> Change without stability is but chaos and stability without change is death.
> —Alfred North Whitehead

The stress of change can be managed better, as noted, when group development is encouraged.

Change must be supported continuously through all stages. Support is motivating, especially during difficult times.

Keep everyone informed. This task may be difficult when large numbers of people are involved in community building, but it is imperative.

Treat surprises and failures as opportunities to learn instead of as disasters. This makes it more acceptable for group members to take risks and grow.

Empower group members by giving them authority and responsibility to make decisions. The old saying, "If you want it done right, do it yourself," represents an attitude that disempowers people. Empowerment in building resilient communities models preferred states and helps people move toward shared values and purposes.

Leaders must support their words with appropriate actions. People believe in leaders who do what they say they are going to do.

> Three-fourths of the miseries and misunderstandings in the world will disappear if we step into the shoes of our adversaries and understand their standpoint.
> —Gandhi

Many leaders hesitate to share authority and control, particularly if they doubt that others share their values and goals. This may be understandable, but it gets in the way of reciprocal influence and empowerment, which are critical elements in resiliency building.

Stronger communities are developed through opportunities for leadership development around meaningful goals and action plans. People must know that their leaders value their participation and care about, support, and trust them. In other words, leaders need to facilitate inclusion.

Facilitation Skills

Good facilitation skills need to be practiced by leaders and other participants. The intention of this section is to summarize key facilitation areas that can enable or inhibit community resiliency development efforts.

Volumes have been written about facilitation skills, (e.g., Johnson & Johnson, 1991; Napier & Gershenfeld, 1993; Schmuck & Runkel, 1994). The following discussion is by no means comprehensive. Rather, it is intended only to suggest ways of avoiding many of the problems that might otherwise arise during resiliency development efforts by focusing on facilitation of the process. Facilitation skills that are particularly important regarding resiliency initiatives are vision building and goal setting, communication, problem solving, decision making, managing meetings, and conflict management.

Vision Building and Goal Setting

Vision building for a resilient community should be about examining and clarifying beliefs and putting these beliefs into the context of a better future for the community. Building a vision should not be done by a select few or reserved for formal leaders. Widespread dialogue about beliefs needs to take place before vision statements are written. It takes time and reflection to formulate a clear and agreed-on vision. Fullan (1993) reminds us that "under conditions of dynamic complexity one needs a good deal of reflective experience before one can form a plausible vision. Vision emerges from, more than it precedes, action" (p. 28). Given adequate time for this activity, vision building for a resilient community can be a powerful and driving force.

An effective way to begin might be to have participants share their views about the community. This exploration can reveal how each participant feels about the community and his or her vision of what it can become. With each participant's personal vision shared, meaning can be established because personal visions are reflections of valued beliefs.

As important, similarities of beliefs can be clarified through such discussions and shared visions can emerge from such interactions between members of the community. Senge (1990) stated it succinctly when he described shared visions as being vital for development of learning communities. Vision statements focus energy for learning. Generative learning occurs only when people are striving to accomplish something that matters deeply to them. In fact the whole idea of generative learning— "expanding your ability to create"—will seem abstract and meaningless *until* people become excited about some vision they truly want to accomplish" (p. 206). The emphasis is on *shared* visions: "people with a strong sense of personal direction can join together to create a powerful synergy toward what I/we truly want" (p. 211).

The process is as important as the product when it comes to understanding and building ownership of a vision. The forming, shaping, and reshaping of a vision builds ownership. The community must experience the process of creating a vision before understanding and ownership can be developed.

> Creating a vision forces us to take a stand for a preferred future.
>
> —P. Block

Different paths for arriving at goals and action plans can be taken during the process. A typical sequence would be to create belief statements, a vision statement, a mission statement, and goals that are agreed on by the group. Each step of the process continuously narrows the focus and more clearly defines the direction in which the community wants to go.

A mission statement, which has to do with intent or purposes, is based on the vision. When decisions are made about using resources and energies, they should support the mission statement. Goals are derived from vision and mission statements and provide more specific directions for action. Keep them focused and limited. Generally speaking, four to six goals may be all that are manageable. People who will be expected to operationalize goals should be included in their development. Including key stakeholders is necessary throughout the process.

Strategies to Help With Vision Building, Mission Statements, and Goal Settings

- Involve community representatives. Building a shared vision cannot be a top-down activity.
- Encourage leaders to listen to views of others and be prepared to modify and adapt visions accordingly.
- Recognize that there may be tensions between participants when a vision is being developed. Embrace and incorporate the diversity of views and develop ways to channel these tensions so they strengthen the vision.

Communication

"Inquiring minds want to know" is a message that needs to be heeded, particularly when it comes to initiating something as different and as complicated as building community resiliency. Inadequate information sharing or waiting too long to share information are pitfalls to be avoided, especially given the complexity of getting relevant information into the hands of participants in most communities. Messages that are clearly articulated, involve key stakeholders, build understanding, and develop ownership require effective communication practices.

Covey (1989) identified communication as one of seven effective habits. The essence of this particular habit is to seek to understand and then to be understood. This requires effective practice of good communication skills. For example, paraphrasing is important to ensure understanding, descriptions of behaviors help pinpoint what is observed, and sharing feelings helps members understand how others perceive things and what motivates them (Schmuck & Runkel, 1994). However, more often than not, communications are handled in expedient and efficient ways but not necessarily effective ways. Focusing on efficiency in communication often leads to information giving rather than active listening and sharing.

> **Seek not to understand that you may believe, but believe that you may understand.**
> —*Saint Augustine*

The critical point is to communicate clearly, regularly, and frequently because people go through the stages of change at different times and information can easily be misinterpreted. Communication takes constant work to be effective, but the effort is important to pursue so that problems can be diminished and the quality of relationships within the community can be improved.

There are three forms of formal communication: *one-way, one-way with feedback,* and *two-way* (Schmuck & Runkel, 1994). When they are used appropriately and effectively, communication can be strengthened. Healthy communication promotes involvement and ownership of vision, mission, and goal accomplishment.

One-way communication (e.g., newsletters, newspapers, memos, and TV and radio notices) can be an efficient way of disseminating information that does not require feedback. This form of communication is useful when information is routine and content is understood and agreed on. In such situations, using valuable resources, people, and time to conduct a dialogue is not required to keep everyone informed. However, one-way communication is inappropriate when information is about nonroutine matters that require discussion and buy-in.

One-way communication with feedback (e.g., surveys, tear-off sheets, and encouragement of paraphrasing to promote understanding) is best used when there is widespread agreement about purposes and actions, but it is important to ensure that members understand the what and how of that which is to be done. It is inappropriate to use one-way communication with feedback when modification and improvement of plans require open discussion or, on the other hand, when information is clear and agreed on, and it is not necessary to get feedback.

Two-way communication (e.g., open dialogue at town meetings, explorations at planning sessions, shared vision building, and discussion about appropriate policies) is an effective way of communicating, but it is costly in terms of the skill and time that is required. This form of communication promotes fluidity between participants when information is being shared. In fact, it may be difficult to tell who is sending and who is receiving information because roles flow back and forth. Two-way communication is most useful when dealing with new initiatives, policy development, and commitment building because the personal contact involved promotes ownership. It is inappropriate to use two-way communication for routine information dissemination, because it is so time consuming and because it is not necessary. For these reasons and because of the time and skills that are required, this method should be used sparingly.

Strategies That Can Enhance Effective Communication

- Use the form of communication that appropriately matches the intended results. The criteria of effectiveness as well as the criteria of efficiency should be considerations during the resiliency-building process.

- Assess the ratio of use of one-way, one-way with feedback, and two-way communication. Generally speaking, the majority of communication should be one-way or one-way with feedback. Two-way communications should be used least frequently and then, only reserved for important issues that require agreement and clarification.

- Give consistent messages to avoid confusion. Furthermore, people frequently need to hear a message two or three times before they can process it.

Problem Solving

Problem solving, a central process in community resiliency building, brings information together about the status quo and focuses on generating proposals for improvement. Problems can be seen as obstacles or opportunities to learn and grow. What matters is how we respond to them. They need to be treated as part of the change landscape—natural and to be expected.

When problems are dealt with superficially, people fight for turf, appearance may become more important than substance, disagreements are likely to be avoided or squelched, blame will probably be laid on those who disagree, and there will likely be resistance to revealing underlying differences (Senge, 1990). Unwillingness to deal with problems reduces chances for improvement. In fact, if change is smooth, proceeding as anticipated without a hitch, it is likely that outcomes will be superficial or trivial. Communities that are serious about becoming healthier need to confront their problems and deal with them effectively.

- Recognize that problems change during the process. An example is members' attitudes about purposes and activities.

- Resist the tendency to delay resolving problems in hopes of attaining full information. Getting all of the information that is desired for problem solving is not likely to occur.

- View problem solving as an ongoing and continuous process because dynamics change and targets shift.

- Establish structures and procedures that encourage periodic checks to determine how problem solving is proceeding.

- See problems as opportunities and acting accordingly. Remember that

> life doesn't follow straight-line logic; it conforms to a kind of curved logic that changes the nature of things. . . . Problems then, are not just hassles to be dealt with and set aside. Lurking inside each problem is . . . a vehicle for personal growth. This entails the need for a shift; we need to value the *process* of finding the solution—juggling the inconsistencies that meaningful solutions entail. (Pascale, 1990, p. 263)

Decision Making

Making decisions is about making choices. The issue for community resiliency building is when to use which decision-making processes for what decisions. There are many forms of decision making, but for present purposes, they can be reduced to three basic formats: decisions by individual persons or small groups, decisions by groups through majority rule,

> Long-range planning does not deal with future decisions, but with the future of present decisions.
>
> —*Peter Drucker*

or group decisions through consensus. Each form has its usefulness, so groups need to think about when each should be practiced.

An individual person or small group can be granted sole authority and responsibility for a decision. This type of decision-making process is efficient and can be appropriate when it is necessary to respond to an emergency situation or when the decision can be delegated because it will be based on previous group agreements or it is a rather routine matter. This decision-making format is inappropriate when decisions are policy related and will have a lasting impact on how the school and community organize and operate or when involvement and ownership are important.

Group decision making by majority rule leaves authority and responsibility for deciding to the group. This type of decision making may be appropriate if efficiency is of the utmost importance, there is limited time, the group is cohesive, or everyone does not have to participate in implementing the decision. However, if the group is divided and agreement is important, majority rule can lead to polarization.

Group consensus decision making is best used when everyone is willing to support the decision even if it is not fully agreeable with him or her. This decision-making approach takes time and requires good communications and conflict management skills, so it needs to be used sparingly. It is best used when full deliberation is important, as is often the case regarding the development of new policies, goals, and procedures. On the contrary, it is inappropriate to practice group consensus building when a decision is routine or mandated, or expertise and skill in decision making is what is most needed.

Another way of viewing low-to-high decision-making involvement has been developed by Tannenbaum and Schmidt (1958):

- Telling: The leader makes the decision
- Selling: The leader makes the decision and tries to persuade others to agree with it
- Testing: The leader presents a proposed decision for group input before making the final decision
- Consulting: The leader asks for input before making decisions and shares the rationale for using or not using the input
- Joining: The leader is an equal member in the group that makes the decisions
- Abdicating: The group makes the decision either because the leader delegates it or by default

Groups need to be involved in making decisions that have to do with building resilient communities. For this to occur, meaningful information must be shared openly, and members need to develop skills required to make decisions as a group. When complex decisions are made as a group, more commitment and motivation are likely to be increased, but this can only happen if proper conditions are established.

Some Strategies for Promoting Effective Decision Making

- Provide decision-making skill development for all group members.
- Encourage group input and participation in decisions.
- Agree on which decision-making format—individual or small group, majority vote, or consensus decision making—is appropriate for which purposes.
- Be aware of unrealistic expectations and accept the fact that decision making about community resiliency building is bound to be a messy affair.

> The hole and the patch should be commensurate.
> —Thomas Jefferson

We have all suffered through frustrating and ineffectual meetings. However, if conducted well, meetings can be an important means of developing and sharing values and purposes, informing members, solving problems, making decisions, and building relationships. The productivity of meetings depends on a number of factors, including clarity of purpose, size of group, time constraints, compatibility of members, status differentials, physical location, and skills of leaders. The frequency of meetings and the time of day they are held also affect meeting effectiveness.

Schmuck and Runkel (1994) identified four features of effective meetings: (a) a balance of task (content) and maintenance (group development), (b) group-orientated agendas, (c) shared leadership, and (d) follow-through.

Creating a balance between task accomplishment and group maintenance promotes effective meetings. People need to believe that they are valued, that they will be able to interact positively and effectively (interpersonal maintenance) at meetings, and that agreed-on tasks will be accomplished. Structures that provide for both maintenance and task accomplishment are necessary. Members can easily derail meetings through confusion or by various forms of misbehavior if group maintenance is not prioritized. Similarly, to function effectively as a group, members need tasks to be specified, and leaders need to encourage follow-through so that decisions will result in meaningful actions.

People who have self-oriented and sometimes hidden agendas that are not addressed will likely exhibit unproductive behaviors, such as blocking, fighting, sandbagging, and withdrawing. To promote a group orientation, time must be given to resolve issues that have created disturbances to the group's work so that energy can be focused on goal achievement.

Shared leadership distributes meeting functions so that more members get to participate effectively and burdens are shared. Leadership can be shared regarding planning and other preparation activities, building agendas based on goals, coordinating tasks, keeping records, promoting positive interpersonal dynamics, giving feedback, evaluating the effectiveness of meetings, and planning for follow-up activities. In short, shared leadership can result in greater participation and group ownership of goals and activities.

> No one is useless in this world who lightens the burdens of another.
> —*Charles Dickens*

Follow-through is necessary after meetings. Follow-through includes getting previous meeting minutes processed and distributed, getting tasks moving and completed, and preparing for future meetings. Fast and consistent follow-through builds confidence among group members as well as trust with the leadership.

Some Strategies to Make Meetings More Effective

- Honor those who come on time by starting on time.

- Set a time frame for conducting business.

- Distribute agendas in advance so that people can be prepared.

- Arrange the room to match the purposes of the meeting. An informational meeting can be set up theatre style, with presenters using visuals to explain key points. If interaction is important, the room and seats should be set up so that face-to-face discussions can take place (e.g., in a circle, a rectangle, or small groups around tables).

- Finish at the agreed-on stopping time. Time is precious for everyone.

Conflict Management

Conflicts are inevitable. Moreover, they often provide the impetus for growth and breakthroughs. Conflicts can range from misunderstandings or disagreements over important issues to emotionally charged struggles over limited resources.

Conflicts that are brought out into the open and dealt with effectively can often be resolved, and the performance of individuals and group members can be strengthened. But this requires that trust and constructive openness is in place. Most people are not accustomed to open confrontation of conflicts, especially given the diversity that exists in most communities. Confronting conflicts in such situations requires facilitation skills.

> It is one of the beautiful compensations of life that no man can sincerely try to help another without helping himself.
> —Ralph Waldo Emerson

Different types of conflict require different responses. There are alternative ways of categorizing conflicts. Schmuck and Runkel (1994) identify three types of conflicts: *Factual conflicts* occur when there is disagreement over facts or there is unequal distribution of information about them. Some facts can be determined easily, such as the number of buildings that exist in the school district, but some are more difficult to discern, such as opinions held about the health of the community. *Strategy conflicts* occur when there is disagreement over the best methods to use to accomplish a goal. *Value conflicts* can be quite intense because they occur when there is disagreement about beliefs and values.

George Carney proposed four types of conflict and effective strategies for dealing with them. These conflicts and his proposed solutions are illustrated in Table 7.1. The important thing is to diagnose what kind of conflict is occurring and develop responses that fit the situation.

TABLE 7.1   Conflicts: Sources and Responses

Sources of Conflict	*Solutions*
• Meaning of words: Language may not be understood or may hold different meaning for different individuals.	• Clear up meaning: Make sure everyone understands the terms that are used.
• Evidence: People may have different information, or some members may have access to more information.	• Get the same information to everyone: Provide it in understandable terms.
• Reasoning processes: People may reason differently, based on their own unique experiences, thought patterns, and so on.	• Check reasoning: Have members share their reasoning with each other.
• Values: People may hold deeply felt and different values.	• Agree to disagree: If it is okay that all do not agree, recognizing differences can promote care and respect. If disagreement is not possible, it may be necessary to separate those involved.

SOURCE: Adapted from G. Carney (personal communication, May 1979).

Some Strategies for Managing Conflict

- Collect data about conflicts from a variety of sources and use different methods, including questionnaires, interviews, and observations.

- Devise procedures and rules for resolving conflicts that everyone can agree with *before* conflicts arise.

- Clarify the issues and confront them until they are resolved. This may intensify them temporarily but, usually, covering up conflicts only makes them worse.

- Recognize that new experiences can bring out the worst in people (e.g., greed for power, autocratic styles of leadership, exclusionary behaviors, and heightened fears of the unknown).

- Conduct periodic reviews to keep the process in balance.

- Look below the surface for the potential of hidden conflicts.

- Decide if the tension that is created by the conflict enhances productivity or inhibits it.

- Determine whether the conflict interferes with the group's goals. If it does not, confrontation may be unnecessary or can at least be delayed.

- Determine if those in conflict really need to work together. If not, separating them may be sufficient.

- Create structural responses—reorganizing, modifying, or shifting roles; increasing resources; and changing schedules.

Assessment, Monitoring, and Evaluation

> There is something I don't know
> that I am supposed to know.
> I don't know what it is I don't know,
> and yet am supposed to know.
> And I feel I look stupid
> if I seem both not to know it
> and not know *what* it is I don't know.
> Therefore, I pretend I know it.
> This is nerve-wracking since I don't
> know what I must pretend to know.
> Therefore, I pretend I know everything.
>
> —*R. D. Laing*

Assessment, monitoring, and evaluation are activities that can help identify and determine successes and failures of efforts to improve school and community resiliency. Unfortunately, these activities are often developed post facto instead of as an ongoing process to establish how well resources are invested.

Clarity is needed about the purpose of information gathering. Is it for accountability? Determination of program worth? Knowledge building and sharing? Capacity building? Or is it for other reasons? The purposes of assessment, monitoring, and evaluation should be to strengthen the process of resiliency building by providing information that can guide the community toward greater health. Knowing what is and what is not

> Research is to see what everybody else has seen, and to think what nobody else has thought.
> —*Albert Szent-Gyorgyl*

working well is important information for such growth. However, many people—leaders most of all—fear such scrutiny. If this fear is not responded to effectively, the initiative may wander off target and self-serving judgments can take the place of meaningful feedback about the status quo, progress, and outcomes.

The rest of the chapter focuses on assessment, monitoring, and evaluation, including practical methods of making these methods work in diverse situations. We discuss efficient and effective ways of collecting, analyzing, and reporting findings for review and decision making in the policy arena.

Meaningful assessment and monitoring (formative information gathering) and evaluations (summative information gathering) require clearly defined purposes and time lines, as well as the skillful use of appropriate information gathering methods. How we know that resiliency-building plans are actually followed and supported is through assessment, monitoring, and evaluation.

Assessment

Assessment is about clarifying and agreeing on starting points: For instance, is the community ready to launch a resiliency-building effort? What are the most critical needs? What are some good vantage points from which to start the effort?

It is also helpful to keep outcomes in mind so information that is gathered can be assessed against intent. Clarifying where you want to go and what the community might look like in the future can be facilitated by using the "Roof" exercises (5.5 and 5.6) introduced in Chapter 5.

There are different ways to assess the initial situation. Selecting tools that are flexible and can improve the possibilities of identifying problems and meaningful goals is a challenge. The important point is that *there is no one right way!* In fact, several complementary methods may be the best approach. A few examples of information-gathering tools and ways of using them follow. For the most part, these tools can be used during all three information-gathering phases—assessment, monitoring, and evaluation.

Assess the current state of community resiliency. This should be done early on. See exercises introduced earlier in the book for straightforward ways of doing these assessments (Exercises 1.1, 1.2, 2.1, 3.1, 6.1, 6.2, 6.3, and 6.4). Doing these exercises in heterogeneous groups can promote widespread involvement of diverse community groups, clarify resiliency concepts and processes, promote ownership and trust, and build the intensity and motivation needed to launch efforts.

Conduct interviews. This is another method for assessing the current state of the community. Probing questions can be asked of individuals to get at in-depth information. People should be encouraged to express their ideas and perceptions if they are going to believe that their opinions matter. It takes time and money to conduct interviews, but the pay-off can make the effort worthwhile.

Conduct focus groups. A group-based interviewing technique, focus groups (Krueger, 1994) can clarify community stakeholders' perceptions. A trained outside facilitator or a committee can be formed, and a set of questions can be developed to guide focus group interviews (group size should be about 6 to 8). Diverse representative groups can be interviewed, probing questions can be asked, layers can be peeled back, and group dynamics can be observed.

Conduct surveys. A survey that addresses the six resiliency factors can be an efficient way of establishing a general sense of community attitudes about issues. After surveys are designed, completed, and returned and results are collated, outcomes can be disseminated to the community. Many people can participate, and important issues can be identified through surveys. Of course, care must be taken about survey item construction, and sampling needs to be representative so results will be accurate and meaningful.

Make observations. Observations can provide reflective feedback on the process. Group dynamics can be observed and analyzed, and suggestions for changes and improvements can be developed.

Analyze documents Analysis of documents can establish what is known and how it is perceived. Useful documents to collect and analyze include school and community demographic summaries and analyses, government agency and voluntary organization publications, as well as clippings from the local newspaper.

Involvement of community members is essential to the information-gathering process to get different perspectives and judgments, as well as to build participation and ownership. Another outgrowth of involving community stakeholders might be more closely shared perceptions.

Monitoring

The purpose of monitoring is to make incremental adjustments so that plans and actions do not go awry. If there are major strengths and pitfalls, it is better to learn about them early so that adjustments can be made, instead of discovering them later through trial and error.

Monitoring is an ongoing process of determining the extent to which goals are being implemented. It is a formative activity, a systematic examination of the process that ensures that results will not be left to chance. Monitoring generates understanding, strategies for improvement, and continued growth.

People want to know where they are going and whether they are actually proceeding along the desired way. If they have a sense of movement, they will be more willing to continue to participate. Therefore, once plans have been set into motion, a system of monitoring progress is critical to success. Achieving a balance between too little and

> If you don't know where you are going, you will probably end up somewhere else.
> —*Laurence J. Peter*

too much monitoring is essential. Monitoring for resiliency development is similar to monitoring factors for the growth of a tree: checking the soil for nutritional value—acidity or alkaline balance, dampness—too much or too little water, the right amount of sunlight, and the availability of wind to strengthen the tree. But pulling the tree out of the ground to check for growth would be detrimental, in much the same way that stopping resiliency building efforts to check for progress would be detrimental.

Benchmarking has become a popular method for monitoring the progress of activities and the level of implementation of initiatives. Benchmarks are predetermined prior to implementation and are based on the best practices that have been established. For present purposes, this means identifying best practices from community resiliency development efforts that are viewed to be successful (see Chapter 8 for a sample of such efforts).

Beyond the tools already presented for information gathering, some other suggestions for monitoring the progress include the following:

- Establish periodic check-ups to understand and assess the process
- Build opportunities into the plan for problem identification
- Procure a trained external evaluator, who can give formative feedback about the process once or twice a year
- Identify potential obstacles and, as they arise, develop alternative plans

Evaluation

The purpose of evaluation is to determine the extent to which goals have been accomplished and to determine the value and worth of efforts that have been made so that policymakers will have information about initiatives on which to base resource allocation decisions. Evaluation is summative in nature—it focuses on outcomes.

Selection of appropriate methods to evaluate resiliency initiatives is critical in determining strengths and areas of growth that are required. Data can be collected in a variety of ways (see methods listed under the Assessment section of the chapter), depending on the purpose and goals of the evaluation. Some suggestions for evaluating efforts include the following:

- Define criteria for evaluation before beginning
- Understand the political forces that may impinge on the evaluation process
- Secure the services of a knowledgeable external evaluator who can advise the community about the best way to proceed
- Conduct evaluations at the end of each phase to serve as a basis for continued improvement

- Recognize that goals and plans for evaluation should be reviewed and developed early rather than waiting until the end of the effort to think about evaluation

Assessment, monitoring, and evaluation are essential activities if we hope to know what is happening and what has been accomplished. Identifying challenges and successes motivates continuing participation by community members. Besides testing progress and documenting out-

> Society is always taken by surprise at any new example of common sense.
> —Ralph Waldo Emerson

comes, assessment, monitoring, and evaluation can build understanding, trust, and ownership in the resiliency-building process. These are a necessity, not an option, if communities are going to be able to move toward increased resiliency. The results of assessment, monitoring, and evaluation can strengthen plans for growth and resiliency.

The final chapter of the book, Chapter 8, provides examples of rural, small town, suburban, and urban communities that have taken the initiative to build resiliency among their members. These communities are taking risks, developing different ways of relating, and achieving results that can be meaningful to other communities that are initiating similar activities. Additional information about other resilient community initiatives, along with helpful resources for managing the process, is also presented in Chapter 8.

Examples of Resilient Communities

Where It's Happening

We must have towns that accommodate different educational groups, different ethnic groups, towns where all can live in one place.

—Margaret Mead

In this final chapter, we turn our attention to communities that have made the commitment to become healthier places to live and work. There are many "real life" examples of communities that are trying to improve resiliency for their members, adults as well as youth, that can provide guidance for your own community's initiatives. The intent of this chapter is to help communities that are ready to take action by showing how others are actively pursuing similar goals.

The chapter is composed of three sections. To provide reality perspectives about limitations and possibilities, the first section summarizes suggestions and insights offered by Lisbeth Schorr (1997), who has studied the efforts and outcomes of many community-based improvement initiatives. The second section provides examples of initiatives being made by small and large communities to improve the quality of their members' lives. It also offers ways of making contact and getting further information about these and similar initiatives. The third section is composed of a diverse sampling of books, compendiums, Web sites, and other resources that provide a rich array of approaches, ideas, and formats that can be employed as your community initiates and conducts improvement efforts.

A Reality Perspective

> A critical mass of Americans has come to understand that mere treatment of symptoms is not an adequate response to the diseases that plague us. We must fundamentally change the way we think.
> —Marrianne Williamson

Lisbeth Schorr (1997) has observed and analyzed some of the most ambitious efforts to improve communities. Her analysis has led her to the conclusion that the most effective programs share seven basic attributes:

Successful programs
1. are comprehensive, flexible, responsive and persevering . . .
2. see children in the context of their families . . . strong families are key to healthy children . . .
3. deal with families as parts of neighborhoods and communities . . .
4. have a long-term, preventive orientation, a clear mission, and continue to evolve over time . . .
5. are well managed by competent and committed individuals with clearly identifiable skills. . . .
6. Staffs . . . are trained and supported to provide high-quality, responsive services . . .
7. operate in settings that encourage practitioners to build strong relationships based on mutual trust and respect. (pp. 5-10)

In an earlier work, *Within Our Reach,* Schorr (1989) surveyed numerous programs that looked quite promising. However, in *Common Purpose* (Schorr, 1997) she reported that within 5 years of these observations, fully half of them were no longer in existence. It is important to assess reasons for the demise of so many good programs, particularly if we hope to improve our chances of successfully initiating and implementing school and community improvement efforts.

Schorr's (1997) conclusion was that most of the time, the programs themselves were not deficient. Rather, it was

the failure to understand that the environment within which these programs have to operate, and which these programs depend on for long-term funding, skilled professionals, and public support, is profoundly out of sync with the key attributes of success. Scaling up effective services requires conditions that are still exceedingly rare. (p. 19)

So long as programs remain small and outside the mainstream of community power structures and government oversight, they have a good chance of persisting. However, the irony is that once they are recognized and valued, they become more involved with resource-granting centers, both public and private, that impose rules and other restrictions that tend to dilute their effectiveness and may eventually lead to their collapse. In short, they are more likely to persist if they stay small and free of entanglements with the very systems that they are trying to influence.

> We must reform if we would conserve.
> —*Franklin Delano Roosevelt*

To get past this pervasive dilemma, initiatives that are attempting to positively affect the resiliency of communities must become more effective in dealing with the systems they want to change. If they are to persist past the "hothouse" stage, Schorr (1997, chap. 9) says that they will need to do these things:

1. Actively seek information about what seems to be working elsewhere so that they gain from these experiences and avoid making unnecessary mistakes.

2. Seek "nontechnical," noncategorized assistance from providers who get up close and personal and are present and available over the long haul to help initiate, implement, and institutionalize improvement efforts.

3. Develop political influence to affect decisions about neighborhoods and communities and mobilize community support for improvement initiatives.

4. Challenge the conditions under which they receive funding (i.e., away from narrow, categorical funding and reporting and toward funding that is more holistic, reflecting the complex goals and priorities that are being pursued).

5. Make a successful case for obtaining more funds from resource providers because the magnitude of the task is well beyond the current resources being set aside for community renewal.

6. Make it clear that failure to provide sufficient support now will likely lead to failures of improvement efforts and thus will increase the need for much larger funding support later (e.g., for police, prisons, court systems, public health systems, and so on).

Schorr's (1997) list of what successful improvement programs need to consider may appear quite daunting. Certainly, it leaves the clear message that such programs need to be thought through carefully and that long-term, broad-based support needs to be obtained if goals are going to have a chance to be institutionalized.

> We do pretty much whatever we want to. Why can't we live in good cities?
> —*Philip Johnson*

The good news is that community improvement champions are becoming much more knowledgeable about what it takes to launch, sustain, and institutionalize change efforts because of the experiences that have been accumulated through earlier efforts. In fact, there are more sustaining efforts being launched than ever before. The increase is due, at least in part, to increasing awareness and readiness on the part of more people in many communities to get involved. There is much that can be learned from these efforts. We encourage you and others to study them as your community gears up for its own resiliency improvement initiatives.

> Nothing ever succeeds which exuberant spirits have not helped to produce.
> —Frederick Nietzche

Communities on the Forefront of Improvement

We know that with sufficient motivation, communities can be mobilized to engage in improvement efforts. For example, communities around the country joined together to cope with Y2K (year 2000) problems associated with computer technology. Town meetings were held and committees were formed, as people joined together for a common cause. Y2K was initially seen as a problem for private and public organizations to solve, but soon it was recognized as everyone's problem and that it had to be solved through collaborative, communitywide efforts (Wheatley & Kellner-Rogers, 1998b). Entire communities rallied together to tackle the problem.

> We need more mass experience, not less. We need more civilized contact with our neighbors, not less.
> —James A. Michener

Community resiliency-building challenges may not be as sharply etched as the Y2K problem, but there is significant evidence that it is becoming a priority focus in many communities around the country. In our review of resiliency-building efforts in rural, small town, suburban, metropolitan, and urban communities, many examples were readily found. This section highlights a few of the efforts that are taking place. The examples we have found range from homegrown to national efforts to help communities, and vary in scope from individual schools and their neighborhoods to large and complex metropolitan population centers. There are far too many community initiatives to attempt any sort of coherent inventory. What we can do is offer a sampling so that readers can get a sense of the variety of initiatives being implemented. We begin with a case description of a community we have worked with, Ashland, Oregon, as it launched a community resiliency effort. Following the case description, we offer a brief sampling of other improvement initiatives going on in towns and cities of different sizes across the country. In addition, we list sources of information that are available to learn more about these and other community improvement efforts.

> Our behavior is a function of our decisions, not our conditions. . . . We have the initiative and the responsibility to make things happen.
> —Stephen Covey

Ashland, Oregon

Ashland, Oregon, a community of approximately 20,000, is the home of Southern Oregon University and the Oregon Shakespeare Festival. Its diverse population includes blue-collar workers, crafts people, merchants, educators, and actors.

In February 1997, 70 people came together at the university for a workshop with us. They explored ways in which the community and the schools could promote resiliency, not just for students but for *all* community members. What occurred that day, and through follow-up activities that have been going on ever since, holds much promise for those interested in promoting resiliency development through interagency collaboration, school and business partnerships, and school-community partnerships.

The activity was initiated by Dr. John Daggett, superintendent of Ashland Public Schools, who believed that the time was ripe to bring all segments of the community together to explore ways that they could work together to move toward greater community resiliency. As he phrased it in the school district's community newsletter,

> Ashland, like the rest of the Rogue Valley, has seen social changes that have the potential of undermining our very special community. Gangs, drugs, violence, teen crime and other compromising factors pose a continual threat to our quality of life as a community. Resiliency training offers a means by which the entire Ashland community—including school, business, church, and other civic entities—may join together to fortify our patrons, and especially our children and youth, against these factors. (Ashland School District, 1996, p. 5)

The people who came together at the university represented a cross-section of the community. They included representatives of the clergy, chamber of commerce, service organizations, social service agencies, city government (e.g., the mayor, police chief, and fire chief), university, treatment and health centers, and students and educators—teachers, counselors, and site-based administrators, as well as the superintendent and other central office administrators. The head of the local teachers' union, which provided major support for the event, also participated.

After the group learned about the six resiliency factors, they were asked to apply them to current efforts under way to respond to needs in the Ashland community. These community members were able to understand the basic meaning of resiliency and that, although Ashland already had a number of resiliency-related activities going on, there was still plenty of room for better coordination. They also came to an agreement about the existence of gaps in current efforts and the need to consider implementing additional initiatives. Last, they expressed concern about the need to broaden the base of support and involvement beyond that of the people in the room.

Equally important, they quickly grasped the importance of shifting the focus from at-risk, which can potentially lead to self-fulfilling prophecies of failure, to a focus on resiliency, which emphasizes supporting everyone's potential for success, whether one is referring to students, educators, or other adult community members.

> None of us is as smart as all of us.
> —Ken Blanchard

They then came to agreement about a commonly held vision of community resiliency that has enabled them to overcome their initial differences. With some facilitation, they were able to visualize what a resilient community might look like in Ashland and identified a number of creative activities that they were willing to commit their time and resources to in pursuit of this vision (e.g., annual celebrations, community potlucks, multimedia dissemination of resiliency concepts and activities, community fairs, town meetings, and awareness and training in safety issues). Last, they recognized the need to institutionalize resiliency initiatives through such activities as ongoing training, stronger focus on prevention, community consensus building, and pursuit of partnerships.

> And in today already walks tomorrow.
> —Samuel Taylor Coleridge

The next day, a smaller group, representing the diverse elements in attendance at the first day's activities, met to develop goals and plans to support making Ashland a more resilient community. Outcomes of this initiative included a commitment to pursue community-based activities that promote resiliency as well as an agreement from the school district's central office and several of the district's schools to focus on resiliency for students and educators. The group also finalized and disseminated its own definition of a resilient community to guide future actions:

A resilient community is comprised of people who bond together, support one another, take responsibility for their actions, are proactive about preparing for the future, and spring back from adversity.

The planning group decided to establish an ongoing group, open to community membership, to keep the momentum going and to guide planning for continuing resiliency development initiatives. A title was created, "Building a Resilient Community (BARC)," and in short order, a mission statement was developed: "To build a safer and healthier community." After some discussion, four goals were also established:

1. Increase the community's knowledge about resiliency
2. Increase the number of opportunities for participation in intergenerational activities

3. Strengthen ties within neighborhoods
4. Expand the use of the school as a community resource center

These goals have been helpful because they have allowed BARC to focus its attention on obtaining necessary resources. They also set a direction for priority activities, clarified expected outcomes, and helped the group identify and differentiate strategies to implement for individuals, families, schools, work sites, and the community in support of these goals.

As BARC initiated its activities, it soon discovered that, in addition to energy and goodwill, it required skills to communicate its vision and facilitate community dialogue. To help build confidence and skill levels, BARC sponsored a "Mentor Training" day in April 1998. At that session, 47 community members—varying from high school students to working adults and retired persons, from age 16 to age 92—learned basic facilitation skills, including how to set goals, develop plans, make presentations, run meetings, and manage conflict. They also learned how to monitor and evaluate their efforts so they could improve on them as they continued to promote resiliency in the community.

BARC, whose membership is a good cross-representation of the community, continues to provide the leadership for community resiliency-building initiatives in Ashland. In fact, it has been expanded in membership and taken on an ever-broader set of activities. As an example of the scope of its initiatives, BARC completed the following activities during a limited time—February and March of 1999:

> It is man's destiny to ponder on the riddle of existence and, as a by-product of his wonderment, to create a new life on the earth.
>
> —*Charles F. Kettering*

Presentations: Presentations were organized and made to acquaint the community with the concept of resiliency. A sample of these activities included three programs on a local TV station about resiliency, the integration of resiliency and special education, and resiliency and technology; presentations about resiliency concepts to local groups at a local library and at Southern Oregon University; the superintendent and two other BARC members facilitated a "Family Action Plans" night at an Ashland elementary school; BARC members made presentations on community resiliency at a local church and to the Ashland Methodist Men's group; and BARC held two monthly meetings.

Communications: A half-page ad about BARC's goals and activities was placed in the local paper, and the March BARC agenda was mailed a full month ahead of the meeting date so that members could be prepared to have a serious discussion and make decisions.

Stimulating new ways of thinking: The videotape, "Finding Our Role in Resilient Communities," by Margaret Wheatley and Robert Theobald (1999) was shown to BARC members and others; a "Parenting Class on Resiliency" was offered at a local library; and BARC sponsored a "Healthy Community/Healthy Youth" asset-building session.

Training: A "speakers bureau" meeting and a speakers and facilitators training workshop were held to help BARC members prepare for speaking engagements and group facilitation.

Negotiating connections: To encourage community participation, BARC was able to get the local ski resort to reduce rates for a day.

In the first years of its existence, BARC's priorities have been to clarify its mission and goals, develop the knowledge and skills necessary to meet them, and increase community awareness, understanding, and involvement in resiliency enhancement activities. With this foundation in place, BARC is preparing to move on to actualizing its long-term mission and goals.

> It's amazing what ordinary people can do if they set out without preconceived notions.
> —*Charles F. Kettering*

A Sampling of Other Community Improvement Efforts

The range of community improvement efforts is broad, as are the priorities and change strategies being implemented in these diverse settings. We offer brief summaries of seven quite different improvement efforts to help readers visualize the scope of what is going on and the alternative approaches that they can consider for their own communities. Because readers may want to access them, after the description we have listed ways of making connections.

Albuquerque, New Mexico, East San Jose Elementary School and Its Neighborhood

The efforts of this urban school of approximately 530 students, which focus on student incentive programs and discipline policy, have been described by Henderson and Milstein (1996). We followed up to see whether the efforts have been sustained. The initiatives that were identified in 1996 are still an important part of school activities. As interesting, a variety of school and community partnerships have subsequently been initiated. According to the principal, Richard Baldonado, these activities include a parent liaison with a family room; a health clinic sponsored by the University of New Mexico Hospital; a human services collaboration; a curriculum that reflects the school and community's goals; outreach efforts for and by students and adults; a partnership with the local community college; and the housing of a 21st-century technology grant for East San Jose's high school cluster, which includes two middle schools, and seven other elementary schools.

Canandaigua, New York

Canandaigua is a rural community of about 10,000 people in upstate New York. The school district and the community have linked together to develop the character of the youth. Various agencies in the community partner with the school district. According to the superintendent, the school district functions as a "clearinghouse for ideas and facilitates the network" (S. Uebbing, personal communication, February 1998). The five character traits that are being focused on are: respect, responsibility, caring, honesty, and healthful lifestyles. Representatives from the school district and community organizations sign an agreement to be partners in promoting these character traits and agree to model exemplary behaviors by displaying them in their own interactions with others. The school district and community have also agreed on ways of implementing plans to teach and model these character traits. Superintendent Uebbing concluded that "without the link to the community, this partnership would not be possible" (S. Uebbing, personal communication, February 1998).

Nampa, Idaho

Nampa, a town of more than 30,000 people near Boise, has experienced rapid population growth. The residential base ranges from families whose breadwinners are employed in local high-tech industries to those who are migrant workers. An impetus to look at the community and how its quality of life could be improved has been accelerated by its unprecedented growth.

The community's leaders decided to take a proactive approach to the escalating demands being placed on their community, especially the schools. They began with a community meeting that attracted "people representing pivotal spheres of influence," which, in turn, led to the decision to start "off with a bold project that could unify the entire community." (Tyler, 1996, p. 9). The Search Institute, whose efforts have been described in Chapters 3 and 6, surveyed the community and found that, similar to findings in many other communities, Nampa's youth were engaging in risky behaviors. Participants asked tough questions, created a vision for their community, and developed a plan to accomplish it. As a result of about 8 years of work, they have been able to bring extensive energy and resources to improve the situation for the youth and for the community as a whole. The focus has been on building trust, listening, reaching out, and developing partnerships. Building a healthier community has also centered on strengthening the family unit as a key building block (Tyler, 1996).

Charleston, South Carolina

Charleston's efforts began with a vision and the leadership of the mayor of 25 years, Joseph P. Riley. The focus of the community's efforts has been on building its future through young people, creating more equality for everyone, reducing crime, providing attractive housing for all, creating green space for serenity, supporting the fine arts, and recognizing the humanity of others, all of which require collaboration. By confronting the ills of this city of approximately 300,000 residents, "Charleston has emerged as a model 'healthy' city in terms of racial harmony and equality, safety, downtown revitalization, housing, beauty, and culture" (Mycek, 1998, p. 10). Latent sources of energy were mobilized as people and organizations that could make a difference were convened to help Charleston become a healthier community. Mayor Riley, based on his extensive community development experience, concludes that

> I've learned that you have to worry about the person in the meager circumstances in your community. You have to fret about the quality of life. If the neighborhood is safe, everyone will feel safe. . . . If you're seeking to achieve that for everyone, if you're worried that anyone is falling through the cracks, then the end result is going to be that you have a healthier, higher quality of life for everyone. . . . The power is in everyone working together. . . . There is nothing in our community that we can't change. (Mycek, 1998, p. 13)

Communities in Schools (CIS) in Charlotte, North Carolina

Communities in Schools (CIS), which provides support to over 200 communities across the nation, has been operating in Charlotte for more than a decade. The mission of CIS is to develop partnerships that connect appropriate services with at-risk youth in specifically identified areas. Unlike many programs, CIS brings assistance to young people instead of requiring them to seek these services. The focus of the Charlotte initiative has been on recruiting caring people and local organizations to help youngsters and their parents. The goals are to prevent dropout and improve self-esteem. Charlotte boasts over 900 volunteers, tutors, and mentors. Rather than just focusing on crisis intervention, a broad range of services is made available. Charlotte has school-based site coordinators in four elementary, nine middle, and six high schools and involves over 70 agencies in the efforts. Cornerstones of the program include early involvement of key stakeholders and recognizing the need to deal comprehensively with the problems of young people and their families. Sustainability has been promoted through community-based ownership, accessibility, and flexibility, which are realized through individualized plans for children and families, key stakeholder involvement and support, and a vision of a healthy community (National Network for Family Resiliency, 1997).

Center for Urban Research and Extension (CURE) in Memphis, Tennessee

The thrust of CURE is to involve University of Memphis faculty and students with local organizations in a citywide effort to build a stronger and healthier community. It is a comprehensive way of thinking about building a healthier city of more than a million residents while developing sustaining relationships that are beneficial to everyone involved. University of Memphis Professors Stan Hyland and David Cox took the university's mission—to be an urban university—seriously when they created the framework for CURE. The projects that have grown out of their initial thinking focus on unemployment, poverty, housing, crime, health, and schools. For example, one project has involved a partnership between the university and the Memphis Housing Authority (MHA). The essence of this project has been to develop collaborative efforts with the residents, local organizations, MHA, and the university in such areas as strategic planning and coordinated social support services. Faculty and students meet with residents to learn about their perceptions of issues, and then experts get involved (e.g., economists address resource aspects and political scientists focus on existing and needed policies). CURE has been a comprehensive way of identifying local issues and bringing appropriate resources to bear to mitigate them. Other projects have included accessing data and using technology to address community issues (e.g., computer mapping so that residents can visualize where high-crime areas, safe areas, and vacant lots are), a plan to promote partnerships to improve the services of a local hospital, and updating a homeless study to gain a clearer picture about this segment of the community so that policies can be recommended and resources can be identified to improve the situation. The design has created a learning community for everyone involved, as the work is done *with* the community, not *to* the community. The community accesses needed resources, community members work collaboratively for a common purpose, and the university participates in ways that emphasize purposeful interventions as well as research (S. Hyland, personal communication, March 1999; Seago, 1997).

American Association of School Administrators (AASA)

AASA has been coordinating a project that involves leading business and philanthropic organizations to help communities across the nation become healthier and stronger. This effort stems from a belief that schools are an integral part of the community and that if they work with others as partners, we can strengthen our nation's schools and communities. AASA is also developing liaisons with organizations around the country to focus on assisting schools and communities partner for the greater health of both.

We have found many examples of communities that are accepting the challenge to address changing realities. We are certain that there are many others that are making comparable efforts but may be too busy to publicize them or may even have purposefully chosen to avoid the limelight and the complications that may accompany it.

The examples we have cited vary not only in community size but in how they have pulled together to build stronger and healthier communities. What is common across these communities is that they are continuing to grow and become more resilient because in each of them, there is a critical mass of citizens who believes that partnering is critical to the future of young people and others. This common belief is the foundation on which they have set up structures and frameworks to address issues.

> We know what we are, but know not what we may be.
>
> —William Shakespeare

Ways of Contacting the Community Initiatives Discussed

Ashland, Oregon:
Ms. Sue Graham, BARC Coordinator
PO Box 3043
Ashland, OR 97520

East San Jose Elementary School, New Mexico:
Mr. Richard Baldonado, Principal,
415 Thaxton Avenue SE
Albuquerque, NM 87102

Canandaigua, New York:
Dr. Stephen Uebbing, Superintendent
Canandaigua City School District
143 N. Pearl
Canandaigua, NY 14424-1496

Nampa, Idaho:
Healthy Nampa, Healthy Youth, Idaho
Chamber of Commerce
208/466-4641

Charleston, South Carolina:
Mayor's Office
City of Charleston
P.O. Box 652
Charleston, SC 29402
843/740-2504

Communities in Schools, Charlotte, NC:
Cynthia B. Marshall, Executive Director
525 N. Tryon St., Suite 200
Charlotte, NC 28202

CURE, Memphis, Tennessee:
Dr. Stan Hyland
Center for Urban Research Extension
127 Fogelman Center
University of Memphis
Memphis, TN 38152

American Association of School Administrators:
Janet Lanigan
1801 North Moore Street
Arlington, Virginia 22209-1813

Additional Resources for
Community Improvement Initiatives

There are many resources for community improvement, some of which describe projects that are working diligently to make a difference and others that provide ideas, strategies, and techniques that can be quite helpful. The following list provides brief summaries about them and how they can be accessed (sites and addresses) for your community's efforts; several excellent resource publications are also included.

America's Promise
909 N. Washington Street
Alexandria, VA 22314
A national initiative based on five resources: ongoing relationship with an adult, healthy start, safe places and structured activities, marketable skills, and opportunities to serve

At Home in Our Schools: A Guide to Schoolwide Activities That Build Community (Child Development Project)
Child Development Project
2000 Embarcadero, Suite 305
Oakland, CA 94606
A book of ideas and strategies aimed at parents, teachers and administrators for implementing schoolwide activities

Building Communities From the Inside Out: A Path Toward Finding and Mobilizing a Community's Assets (Kretzmann & McKnight, 1993)
The Asset-Based Community Development Institute
Institute for Policy Research
Northwestern University

2040 Sheridan Road
Evanston, IL 60208-4100
> *A guide for communities and schools to use to locate assets, skills, capacities of citizens, associations, and organizations*

Center for Community Partnerships
Dr. Ira Harkavy
133 South 36th Street, Suite 519
Philadelphia, PA 19104-3246
> *More than a dozen comprehensive community schools have been created in West Philadelphia by the Center*

Common Purpose: Strengthening Families and Neighborhoods to Rebuild America (Schorr, 1997)
> *A book that we refer to regularly about building communities; many community improvement projects described*

Communities in Schools (CIS)
J. Neil Shorthouse, President
1252 West Peachtree Street, Suite 430
Atlanta, GA 30309
> *A program that brings community resources together to increase literacy, reduce tardiness and absences, and prevent dropouts*

Community Collaboration for Children and Youth
National Association of Counties
440 First Street, NW
Washington, DC 20001-2080
> *A compendium of awards for excellence in community collaboration for children and youth projects throughout the country. Outstanding projects selected each year*

Connecting the Dots: Progress Toward the Integration of School Reform, School-Linked Services, Parent Involvement and Community Schools (Lawson & Briar-Lawson, 1997)
Educational Renewal
McGuffey Hall
Miami University
Oxford, OH 45056
> *Resource includes a model, "The Family-Supportive Community School," with 10 strategies for community improvement*

Community Update
U.S. Department of Education
Washington, DC 20202-0498
> *Free national newsletter that focuses on community involvement*

Compact for Learning and Citizenship
707 17th Street, Suite 2700
Denver, CO 80202-3427

Goals: to engage students in service learning and to maximize community volunteer efforts; sponsored by the Education Commission of the States, focuses on helping schools with service and volunteerism

Employers, Families and Education
Partnership for Family Involvement in Education
600 Independence Avenue, SW
Washington, DC 20202-8173

Strategies published by U.S. Department of Education; focuses on partnerships for family involvement in education through employers, families, and schools

Everybody's House—The Schoolhouse: Best Techniques for Connecting Home, School and Community (Warner, 1997)

Strategies for schools to use to involve the community

First Day of School Holiday (First Day Foundation, annually)
First Day Foundation
PO Box 10
Bennington, VT 05201-0010

Strategies for helping schools, teachers, employers, parents, and students enhance parents' positive involvement with their children's education through newsletter and booklet

Keeping Schools Open As Community Learning Centers: Extending Learning in a Safe, Drug-Free Environment Before and After School
Partnership for Family Involvement in Education
Copies and further information can be obtained through
1-800-USA-LEARN

A booklet of strategies for school and community to use school facilities in ways that extend the educational program for students, jointly sponsored by the National Community Education Association, U.S. Department of Education, Policy Studies Associates, and American Bar Association Division of Education

Learn and Live (The George Lucas Educational Foundation, 1997)
The George Lucas Educational Foundation, Patty Burness,
  Executive Director
PO Box 3494
San Rafael, CA 94912

Information about pioneering improvement efforts; includes a book and a video with ideas, strategies, stories, and resources; geared for community or school use or both

National Center for Community Education
1017 Avon Street
Flint, Michigan 48503

A compendium of community-school partnerships that are making a difference across the country, including comprehensive information about these communities and their programs

National Center for Schools and Communities
Joy G. Dryfoos
Fordham University
33 West 60th Street, 8th Floor
New York, NY 10023
   A resource for information about different initiatives occurring nationwide

*Positive Actions for Living: A Guide for Learning Parent, Family, Community,
and Personal Positive Actions*
Carol Gerber Allred, President/Developer
321 Eastland Drive
Twin Falls, ID 83301
   *A model for comprehensive school reform that was accepted by the U.S.
   Department of Education Title I office for the Catalog of School Reform Models;
   comprehensive approach for involving the community with the school*

Project Change: Educational Equity in Albuquerque, NM
505/242-9536
   *Focuses on creating equity for students of color through a community-based
   approach*

Promising Initiatives to Improve Education in Your Community
Education Publications Center
U.S. Department of Education
PO Box 1398
Jessup, MD 20794-1398
   *A minicatalog of programs and free publications published by U.S. Department
   of Education*

Promoting Your School: Going Beyond PR (Warner, 1994)
   *A guide for schools to use to develop effective public relations with the
   community*

Reaching All Families: Creating Family-Friendly Schools
(Moles, Ed. August 1996)
Office of Educational Research and Improvement
U.S. Department of Education
600 Independence Avenue SW
Washington, DC 20202-8173
   *Strategies and resources for school administrators and teachers to involve
   parents and families as active participants in children's education*

School, Family, and Community Partnerships: Your Handbook for Action
(Epstein, Coates, Salinas, Sanders, & Simon, 1997)
   *A comprehensive framework for developing and implementing school, family,
   and community partnerships; useful for community or school planning or both*

Show Me the Evidence! Proven and Promising Programs for America's Schools
(Slavin & Fashola, 1998)

Reviews major reform efforts at the elementary and secondary school levels for their effectiveness in terms of student achievement and district-level strategies for introducing proven programs

Study Circles Resource Center
PO Box 203
697 Pomfret Street
Pomfret, CT 06258
Education kit and guide for involving the community in initiating participatory discussion on education through study circles; communities and schools can find good uses for these materials.

Web Sites

Building a Collective Vision.
http://www.ncrel.org/skrs/areas/issues/educatrs/leadrshp/le100.htm
A North Central Educational Laboratories website about resiliency.

Building Communities of Support for Families.
http://www.hec.ohio-state.edu/famlife/nnfr/ctf/curricul/13.html

Child and Family Resiliency Research Programme.
http://www.quasar.ualberta.ca/cfrrp/cfrrp.html

Coalition for Healthier Cities and Communities.
http://www.healthycommunities.org

Coping and Resilience.
http://nncf.unl.edu/annie.coping.html

Creative Partnerships for Prevention.
http://www.cpprev.org/contents.htm

Family Resiliency Iowa.
http://www.exnet.iastate.edu/Pages/communications/Resiliency/homepage.html

Human Development and Family Life Bulletin.
http://www.hec.ohio-state.edu/famlife/bulletin/bullmain.htm

iCONNECT.
http://web.aces.uiuc.edu/iconnect/

The Mid Kids: Riding The Waves from Childhood to Adulthood.
http://www.nwrel.org/nwedu/spring%5F96/page3.html

National Network for Family Resiliency: Building Family Strengths.
http://www.nnfr.org/

Project Resilience.
http://www.projectresilience.com

Resiliency In Action.
http://www.resiliency.com

Search Institute.
http://www.search-institute.org/

In Closing

The significant problems we face cannot be solved by the same level of thinking that created them.

—Albert Einstein

We have tried to capture a sense of the passion, dedication, and connections that are required to build resilient communities. Regardless of the size of the community, enhanced resiliency can help it to weather almost any storm. As Mayor Giuliani has proved, even a community the size of New York City can be improved.

> In the long run men hit only what they aim at. Therefore they better aim at something high.
> —*Henry David Thoreau*

As unique as each community is, one belief we hold is that community improvement cannot be just another project. An appropriate analogy might be:

If the fish in a stream were dying, we would not assume that we could solve this problem by pulling the fish out of the stream and allowing them to swim in a clean fish tank for 30 minutes each day, returning them to the original system for the remainder of the day. We would begin a systematic search to find out what was causing the fish to die. Solutions might be a combination of cleaning up the stream, educating the users of the stream, and spending money differently to respond to the problem. If the health of the fish were important to us, we would do what was necessary to restore the health of the stream so the fish could thrive. (Taylor, 1995, p. 1)

Like the fish, if we want community members to thrive we need to link all available resources and recognize that the well-being of one community sector is intimately linked with the well-being of all other sectors of our communities. This calls for the development of sustainable partnerships that provide a clear sense of mutual benefit.

Resource A
Handouts

Handout 1

How Resilient Are You?

How resilient are you? Here's a little test to help you get a sense of your own resiliency. Circle the choice that is most true or typical of you for each of the following questions:

1. When you have difficulties, are you more likely to
   a. Confront them immediately by taking an initiative
   b. Get away from the difficulties in hopes they will pass
2. What is your attitude toward leisure time?:
   a. Enjoy reading, learning, and exploring
   b. Ponder your situation and worry about your future
3. When faced with a challenge, do you
   a. Enjoy the challenge of figuring out the dilemmas and making things happen
   b. Let others take the lead
4. Are your work and home environments
   a. Supportive and energizing
   b. Stressful and exhausting
5. Do you believe that
   a. Good things are most likely to happen to you
   b. Bad things are most likely to happen to you
6. Do you believe that the best years of your life are
   a. Yet to come
   b. Behind you
7. Do you
   a. Have a clear sense of purpose about life
   b. Find yourself drifting from year to year without goals
8. How do you feel about your accomplishments and abilities
   a. Proud of your accomplishments and abilities
   b. Not as capable as you could be when coping with challenging situations
9. When going through life's inevitable transitions, do you
   a. Feel at ease with them
   b. Feel unsettled and in need of more time to adjust
10. Do you believe that you
    a. Must earn what you get
    b. Are entitled to rewards that you want

The more "a" responses that you selected, the more likely it is that you exhibit resilient behaviors. These responses indicate that you probably feel good about yourself most of the time and take pride in your accomplishments. You also probably take challenges that come your way as a part of life and work hard to respond to them effectively.

If you chose "b" responses more than "a" responses, you might want to consider making some changes.

First, you may want to work on changing your attitude and behaviors by practicing more positive self-talk, especially if you tend to be critical of yourself.

Second, you may want to observe and talk with people you think are highly resilient to see what you can learn from them.

Third, you may want to read and think about resiliency-related areas such as self-esteem, career development, life stages, and dealing with transitions.

In whatever ways possible, try to learn about and practice the qualities and skills that promote resiliency.

INTERNAL PROTECTIVE FACTORS
Characteristics of Individuals That Promote Resiliency

1. Gives of self in service to others or a cause or both
2. Uses life skills, including good decision making, assertiveness, impulse control, and problem solving
3. Is sociable and has ability to be a friend and form positive relationships
4. Has a sense of humor
5. Exhibits internal locus of control (i.e., belief in self, ability to influence one's environment)
6. Is autonomous, independent
7. Has positive view of personal future
8. Is flexible
9. Has spirituality (i.e., belief in a greater power)
10. Has capacity for connection to learning
11. Is self-motivated
12. Is "good at something," has personal competence
13. Has feelings of self-worth and self-confidence
14. Other:

ENVIRONMENTAL PROTECTIVE FACTORS

Characteristics Modeled by Families, Schools, Communities, and Peer Groups That Promote Resiliency

1. Promotes close bonds
2. Values and encourages education
3. Uses high warmth, low criticism style of interaction
4. Sets and enforces clear boundaries (rules, norms, and laws)
5. Encourages supportive relationships with many caring others
6. Promotes sharing of responsibilities, service to others, "required helpfulness"
7. Provides access to resources for meeting basic needs of housing, employment, health care, and recreation
8. Expresses high and realistic expectations for success
9. Encourages goal setting and mastery
10. Encourages prosocial development of values (such as altruism) and life skills (such as cooperation)
11. Provides leadership, decision making, and other opportunities for meaningful participation
12. Appreciates the unique talents of each individual
13. Other:

SOURCE: Adapted from Henderson and Milstein (1996).

Handout 3

On Any Given Day

- 135,000 children bring a gun to school

- 30 children are wounded by guns

- 10 children die from guns

- 7,742 teens become sexually active

- 623 teenagers get syphilis or gonorrhea

- 2,556 children are born out of wedlock

- 211 children are arrested for drug abuse

- 437 children are arrested for drinking or drunken driving

- 1,629 children are in adult jails

- 1,849 children are abused or neglected

- 3,288 children run away from home

- 2,989 children see their parents divorced

- 6 teenagers commit suicide

- 1,512 teenagers drop out of school

SOURCE: Adapted from Children's Defense Fund (1990).

Milstein and Henry, *Spreading Resiliency: Making It Happen for Schools and Communities.* Copyright © 2000 by Corwin Press, Inc.

CASE A

Girl, age 16, orphaned, willed to custody of grandmother by mother who was separated from alcoholic husband, now deceased. Mother rejected the homely child, who has been proven to lie and steal sweets. Swallowed penny to attract attention. Father was fond of the child. Child lived in fantasy as mistress of her father's household for years. The grandmother, who is widowed, cannot manage four young uncles and aunts in the household. Young uncle drinks, has left home without telling the grandmother his destination. Aunt, emotional over love affair, locks self in room. Grandmother resolved to be stricter with granddaughter because she fears she has failed with her own children. She dresses the granddaughter oddly. She refuses to let her have playmates. Put her in braces to keep her back straight. Did not send her to grade school. Aunt on paternal side of family is crippled, uncle is asthmatic.

CASE B

Boy, senior in high school, has obtained certificate from physician stating that nervous breakdown makes it necessary for him to leave school for 6 months. Boy is not a good all-around student; has no friends; teachers find him to be a problem, developed speech late; has had poor adjustment to school; and father is ashamed of son's lack of athletic ability. Boy has odd mannerisms; makes up his own religion, chants hymns to himself—parents regard him as "different."

CASE C

Boy, age 6, head large at birth. Thought to have had brain fever (meningitis). Three siblings died before his birth. Mother does not agree with relatives and neighbors that the child is probably abnormal. Child is sent to school and is diagnosed as mentally ill by the teacher. Mother is angry—withdraws child from school, saying she will teach him herself.

SOURCE: Unknown

Handout 5

Judgment Test Answers

The three case studies, in the order presented, summarize the youthful years of three exceptional individuals: Eleanor Roosevelt, Thomas Edison, and Albert Einstein.

What would their lives have been like if, out of the best of intentions, they had been labeled "at risk" and channeled into narrow, limited educational tracks?

What adults say and do when making judgments about youngsters does indeed matter! In fact, too often, much of the coping that youngsters have to do is directly related to adult judgments or lack of support (or both)!

Improving Student Resiliency: A Contract

Resiliency Element	Strengths	Areas for Improvement
Prosocial bonding		
Clear and consistent boundaries		
Life skills		
Caring and support		
High expectations		
Meaningful participation		

Signed by: _____ Student   Date: _____

_____ Parent

_____ Teacher

Handout 7

Educator Plateauing Survey

Select the response that best completes each item, using a scale from 1 to 5, with 1 indicating *strongly agree*, 2 indicating *agree*, 3 indicating *undecided*, 4 indicating *disagree*, and 5 indicating *strongly disagree*.

1. ___ The realities of my job come close to matching my initial expectations.
2. ___ I have high professional regard for those in leadership positions in my organization's structure.
3. ___ I feel trapped because I am unable to advance in my organization.
4. ___ My work is satisfying to me.
5. ___ I feel burdened with the many things I am responsible for in my life.
6. ___ I am bored in my current job.
7. ___ I usually start a new day with a sense of enthusiasm.
8. ___ To the extent that I am interested, I have opportunities to advance in my organization.
9. ___ Work is the most important thing in my life.
10. ___ My job is full of repetitive tasks.
11. ___ I feel like I have been passed over when advancement opportunities have occurred in my organization.
12. ___ I can usually find time to engage in leisure activities that I enjoy.
13. ___ I have little interest in advancing within my organization's structure.
14. ___ My life is too predictable.
15. ___ I participate in challenging and meaningful activities in my job.
16. ___ I believe I can achieve my career goals within my organization's structure.
17. ___ I have been in my job too long.
18. ___ I find myself being impatient too often with family and friends.
19. ___ I wish I had more opportunities to advance in my organization so I could do more meaningful work.
20. ___ I know my job too well.
21. ___ I rarely think of my life as boring.
22. ___ Although I would like to advance in my organization, given my abilities, my present position is the highest I can realistically attain in my organization.
23. ___ My job affords me little opportunity to learn new things.
24. ___ I am energized by the challenges and opportunities in my job.
25. ___ I consider myself a risk-taker in my approach to life.
26. ___ Advancing further in my organization's structure would require that I give up many of the things I really like about my current position.
27. ___ I feel I perform successfully in my current job.
28. ___ My family and friends get irritated with me for being more involved with work than I am with other aspects of my life.
29. ___ My life is turning out as well as I hoped it would.
30. ___ I relate career success to promotion within my organization's structure.

Educator Plateauing Survey Scoring Sheet

The numbers in categories A, B, and C correspond to the 30 statements in the Plateauing Survey. Transfer your responses to the blanks provided.

Note: Those numbers that are followed by an asterisk (*) are reverse-scoring items. For these items, a score of 1 should be entered as 5, 2 becomes 4, 3 remains 3, 4 becomes 2, and 5 becomes 1. *Be sure to reverse these items as noted.*

Category A	*Category B*	*Category C*
1. _____	2. _____	5.* _____
4. _____	3.* _____	7. _____
6.* _____	8. _____	9.* _____
10.* _____	11.* _____	12. _____
15. _____	13. _____	14.* _____
17.* _____	16. _____	18.* _____
20.* _____	19.* _____	21. _____
23.* _____	22.* _____	25. _____
24. _____	26. _____	28.* _____
27. _____	30.* _____	29. _____

Category Totals (add each column):   *Plateau Area:*

A = _____   Divide by 10   = _____   Content (work has become routine)

B = _____   Divide by 10   = _____   Structure (organization doesn't offer opportunity for growth or promotion)

C = _____   Divide by 10   = _____   Life (life is too predictable or not fulfilling)

Total = _____   Divide by 30   = _____   Overall plateauing

The higher the score in each category and overall, the higher the level of plateauing. This survey can be used to assess the need for resiliency building in any of the three plateauing categories or regarding overall plateauing.

Handout 9

Barriers to Educator Resiliency

Prosocial Bonding

Education is a lonely business. We work in isolation.

Performance evaluation is based on individual rather than team efforts.

Clear and Consistent Boundaries

Rules and norms may be complex, unclear, unstated, nonexistent, or ever changing: for example, expected time to be at work, service expectations, discipline policies, and state mandates.

Rules are not applied consistently and equitably.

Life Skills

Preservice education is only minimally sufficient to begin with and is soon outdated.

The rate of change is rapid (e.g., knowledge development, technology, and societal changes).

Little time is allowed to learn new skills.

Caring and Support

Little focus is given to regular, meaningful, and supportive feedback.

Little time is available for adults to share and support each other.

High Expectations

Reward systems do not recognize individual efforts.

The dominant message is to "maintain order and discipline" rather than "take risks" and "make things happen."

Group norms focus on minimal effort and output.

Meaningful Participation

Few career development opportunities exist for professional growth or becoming mentors to others.

Role definitions are narrow.

Little time is available to participate.

*My School: Does it Deter or Support
Resiliency Development?*

1. The six resiliency factors are listed in the following table. If you need the definitions, refer to Chapter 1.

2. *To what extent does your school deter or support the development of the six resiliency factors among students, educators, and community members?* Use the following 5-point scale to record your judgment in each of the columns:

   Supports Resiliency   5   4   3   2   1   Deters Resiliency

3. Think about what the school does overall and record your judgment in the "Overall" column.

4. Add any comments you may want that support your judgments.

Resiliency Factors	Students	Educators	Community	Overall	Comments
Prosocial bonding					
Clear and consistent boundaries					
Life skills					
Caring and support					
High expectations					
Meaningful participation					

Handout 11

Examples of a Community Needing Resiliency Improvement

Increase Prosocial Bonding	*Set Clear and Consistent Boundaries*	*Teach Life Skills*	*Provide Caring and Support*	*Set and Communicate High Expectations*	*Provide Meaningful Opportunities to Participate*
People are isolated	Laws are applied inconsistently	There is denial of problems	Few community services are available	Status quo orientation is maintained	Apathy is evident
Streets are unsafe	Few opportunities exists for community input in governance	Poor problem-identifying and problem-solving skills are apparent	There is need for much greater resources than are made available	A sense of hopelessness prevails	The focus is on differences
A culture of fear and discrimination exists	Tension exists among ethnic, racial, and other groups	There is little evidence of cooperation	Absence of partnerships is the rule	Widespread poor self-esteem/self-concept	Minimal infrastructure for citizen input
There is a lack of effective programs	Favoritism is the norm	Ineffective conflict management is common	Individuals feel anonymous	There is little evidence of mutual respect	There is little or no celebration of successes
Little effort to communicate is made	A sense of community is not shared	Teenage pregnancy and other risky behaviors are prevalent	There is an absence of community celebrations	There are few cooperative or cohesive efforts	Few if any community improvement initiatives are undertaken
Lack of trust is common			Leadership is not noticeably visible	There is an absence of community vision	
Factions thrive within the community			Leadership lacks vision		

Examples of a Community With Characteristics of Resiliency

Increase Prosocial Bonding	*Set Clear and Consistent Boundaries*	*Teach Life Skills*	*Provide Caring and Support*	*Set and Communicate High Expectations*	*Provide Meaningful Opportunities to Participate*
Citizens engage in meaningful discourse	Norms for participation and decision making are established	Human services collaborations exist	Widespread collaboration on community projects exists	Community supports positive vision for the future	Many civic clubs exist with broad membership
An infrastructure exists that promotes cooperative efforts	Proactivity and acceptance are practiced	Lifelong learning opportunities are available	Respect for law and order is widespread	Quality of life is a high priority	Volunteerism is encouraged
Celebrations and rituals exist	Participatory governance exists	Intergenerational programs are operating	Intergenerational contacts are made	High standards of acceptable behavior are set	Community vision is shared and pursued
Interorganizational activities are common	Emphasis is on community	Preventive programs that are proactive are widespread	Service to others is encouraged	Family and community spirit is prevalent	Leadership training is available and effective
Community symbols are evident	Regular and clear communications exist	Support groups are established		Recognition for efforts and achievements are common	
Meaningful partnerships are nurtured					
Past and current cultures are celebrated					

Handout 13

Do You Know How Resilient Your Community Is?
(Score Sheet for Exercise 6.1)

Review the two examples of communities needing resiliency and communities with resiliency (Handouts 11 and 12). Think about your community and place an "X" in the column that you think rates its resiliency for each of the six factors. The last column, "Group Score," is a place to record the average scores your group gives each of the six resiliency factors. Please note additional thoughts in the space provided.

Resiliency Factors	*(Low)* 1	2	3	4	5 *(High)*	Group Score
Prosocial bonding						
Clear boundaries						
Life skills						
Caring and support						
High expectations						
Meaningful participation						

Comments:

1. Everyone accepts personal responsibility for building positive personal and relational attitudes and skills, or assets, in youth.

2. The community thinks and acts with everyone, youth and adults, in mind.

3. Values and boundaries for acceptable behaviors are agreed on and modeled by community members.

4. Youth and adults actively reach out to serve others.

5. Families are supported, educated, and encouraged to keep personal and interpersonal asset building a high priority.

6. Youth receive frequent expressed support.

7. Neighborhoods are safe, supportive, and caring.

8. All schools actively promote care, clear and consistent boundaries, and sustained, healthy relationships with adults.

9. Businesses incorporate policies that support family life and embrace asset-building principles for employees.

10. Virtually all 10- to 18-year-olds are involved in one or more groups that hold building personal and community assets as central to their mission.

11. The media (print, radio, television) frequently articulate and support the community's vision and efforts and provide forums to acknowledge and honor individuals and organizations that have taken innovative actions.

12. All adults who work with youth receive training on how to foster asset building.

13. Youth have opportunities to lead and make decisions.

14. Religious institutions use their resources to foster asset building both within their own programs and in the community.

15. The community exhibits long-term and sustained commitment to asset building.

SOURCE: Adapted from Roehlkepartain and Benson (1996).

Handout 15

Developmental Assets

1. Family support
2. Positive family communication
3. Other adult resources
4. Caring neighborhood
5. Caring out-of-home and school climates
6. Parent involvement in out-of-home situations and in schooling
7. Children and youth valued by community
8. Children have roles in family life and are seen as a resource
9. Service to others
10. Safety
11. Family boundaries
12. Out-of-home and school boundaries
13. Neighborhood boundaries
14. Adult role models
15. Positive peer observation, interactions, and influence
16. Expectations for growth and high expectations
17. Creative activities
18. Out-of-home activities, child programs, and youth programs
19. Religious community
20. Positive, supervised time at home
21. Achievement expectation and motivation
22. School engagement
23. Stimulating activity and homework
24. Enjoyment of learning and bonding to school
25. Reading for pleasure
26. Caring
27. Equality and social justice
28. Integrity
29. Honesty
30. Responsibility
31. Healthy lifestyle and sexual attitudes, and restraint
32. Planning and decision-making observation and practice
33. Interpersonal observation, interactions, and competence
34. Cultural observation, interactions, and competence
35. Resistance observation, practice, and skills
36. Peaceful conflict-resolution observation, practice, and competence
37. Personal power
38. High self-esteem
39. Sense of purpose
40. Positive view of personal future

SOURCE: Adapted from Leffert, Benson, and Roehlkepartain (1997).

School and Community: From Reactive to Proactive Relations

	Closed	Tolerant	Involved	Connected	Outreaching
Beliefs	• Locked down mentality	• Grudging acceptance of legitimate, but limited, role of parents in school	• Community support for school sought and encouraged	• Active networking to develop communitywide, comprehensive, integrated programs	• Mutual support and partnerships
Expectations	• Minimal involvement of parents (controlled by school staff) • Limited time set aside for engagement	• Limited and formalized engagement in school affairs for parents and possibly others in community	• Parents and others actively involved • Social agencies encouraged to collaborate on youth-related activities	• Extensive open, flexible and ongoing relationship between community and school	• All community elements represented • Equal access for initiation, involvement, and decision making
Governance structures	• Explicit and detailed policies or rules for parent involvement set by the school	• Advice sought from select group of parents (PTA or PTO) • School-dominated governance and decision making • PTAs or PTOs dominated by educators	• School sets parameters but seeks active involvement with parents and community	• Schools and other agencies focus on youth and meet together regularly to set priorities and monitor activities	• Interagency councils • Nonbureaucratic and fluid structures that promote mutual influence
Communications	• Highly limited and one-way, from school to parents	• Primarily one-way, from school to parents and community	• School-initiated feedback encouraged from parents and community • Invitational and regular to parents and community	• Two-way and formalized with youth-related agencies and other organizations	• Multichanneled • Two-way • Frequent
Resources	• Minimal resources set aside for relationship purposes • Parents or community resources not pursued	• PTA/PTO fund raising for school priorities • Room Mothers or Fathers with limited roles • Focus limited to students and classroom needs	• Resources for the school identified and solicited	• School facilities made available for community use • Community facilities made available for school use	• School personnel and students engaged as community volunteers
Activities	• School calls on parents when student-related problems arise • Formal and limited parent committees	• Structured and limited parent committees • Principal apprises parents and others of school activities	• Students mentored by community members • Volunteers sought for school programs • Social service agencies function in the school	• Shared use of facilities (e.g., meeting rooms, libraries, and computers) • Summer programs developed cooperatively to meet community needs	• Agreed-on joint initiatives that focus on community improvement • Service learning

Milstein and Henry, *Spreading Resiliency: Making It Happen for Schools and Communities.* Copyright © 2000 by Corwin Press, Inc.

Handout 17

Building Resiliency in Our Community: Now and Tomorrow

	Increase Prosocial Bonding	Set Clear and Consistent Boundaries	Teach Life Skills	Provide Caring and Support	Communicate High Expectations	Provide Meaningful Participation
Community as it currently exists						
Community of the future						

The Sense of a Goose

In the fall when you see geese heading south for the winter flying along in "V" formation, you might be interested in knowing what science has discovered about why they fly that way. It has been learned that as each bird flaps its wings, it creates uplift for the bird immediately following. By flying in a "V" formation, the whole flock adds at least 71% greater flying range than if each bird flew on its own.

(People who share a common direction and sense of community can get where they are going quicker and easier because they are traveling on the thrust of one another.)

Whenever a goose falls out of formation, it suddenly feels the drag and resistance of trying to go it alone, and quickly gets back into formation to take advantage of the lifting power of the bird immediately in front.

(If we have as much sense as a goose, we will stay in formation with those who are headed the same way we are going.)

When the lead goose gets tired, it rotates back in the wing and another goose flies point.

(It pays to take turns doing hard jobs—with people or with geese flying south.)

The geese honk from behind to encourage those up front to keep up their speed.

(What messages do we give when we honk from behind?)

Last, when a goose gets sick, or is wounded by gun shot and falls out, two geese fall out of formation and follow it down to help and protect it. They stay with it until it is either able to fly or until it is dead, and then they launch out on their own or with another formation to catch up with their group.

If we have the sense of a goose, we will stand by each other like that.

SOURCE: Unknown.

References

Anthony, E. J., & Cohler, B. J. (Eds.). (1987). *The invulnerable child*. New York: Guilford.

Ashland School District. (1996). Resiliency skills: Building a healthier community. *Reflections, 1*(1), 5.

Bardwick, J. (1986). *The plateauing trap*. New York: American Management Association.

Benard, B. (1991). *Fostering resiliency in kids*. Portland, OR: Western Regional Center for Drug-Free Schools and Communities, Northwest Educational Laboratory.

Bennis, W. (1989). *Why leaders can't lead: The unconscious conspiracy continues*. San Francisco: Jossey-Bass.

Benson, P. L. (1997). *All kids are our kids: What communities must do to raise caring and responsible children and adolescents*. San Francisco: Jossey-Bass.

Benson, P. L., Galbraith, J., & Espeland, P. (1995). *What kids need to succeed*. Minneapolis, MN: Free Spirit.

Berman, P., & McLaughlin, M. (1978). *Federal programs supporting educational change: Vol. 8. Implementing and sustaining innovations*. Santa Monica, CA: RAND.

Blum, D. (1998, May/June). Finding strength. *Psychology Today*, pp. 32-38, 66-70, 72-73.

Blum, R. W., & Rinehart, P. M. (1997). *Connections that make a difference in the lives of youth*. Minneapolis: University of Minnesota, Division of General Pediatrics and Adolescent Health.

Brown, B. L. (1996). *Career resilience* (Digest No. 178). Columbus, OH: ERIC Clearinghouse.

Canfield, J., & Hansen, M. V. (1993). *Chicken soup for the soul*. Deerfield Beach, FL: Health Communications.

Chapman, C. H. (Ed.). (1997). *Becoming a superintendent: Challenges of school district leadership*. Columbus, OH: Merrill/Prentice Hall.

Children's Defense Fund. (1990). *Children 1990: A report card, briefing book, and action primer*. Washington, DC: Author.

Covey, S. R. (1989). *The 7 habits of highly effective people*. New York: Simon & Schuster.

Drucker, P. F. (1998). Introduction: Civilizing the city. In F. Hesselbein, M. Goldsmith, R. Beckhard, & R. F. Schubert (Eds.), *The community of the future*. San Francisco: Jossey-Bass.

Elder, G. H., Liker, K., & Cross, C. E. (1984). Parent-child behavior in the great depression: Life course and intergenerational influences. In T. B. Baltes & O.G. Brim, Jr. (Eds.), *Lifespan development and behavior* (Vol. 6, pp. 109-158). New York: Academic Press.

Epstein, J. L., Coates, L., Salinas, K. C., Sanders, M. G., & Simon, B. S. (1997). *School, family, and community partnerships*. Thousand Oaks, CA: Corwin.

Farrington, D. P. (1989). Long-term prediction of offending and other life outcomes. In H. Wegener, F. Loesel, & J. Haisch (Eds.), *Criminal behavior and the justice system* (pp. 26-39). New York: Springer.

Fullan, M. (1985). Change process and strategies at the local level. *The Elementary School Journal, 84*(3), 391-420.

Fullan, M. (with Stiegelbauer, S.). (1991). *The new meaning of educational change* (2nd ed.). New York: Teachers College Press.

Fullan, M. (1993). *Change forces: Probing the depths of educational reform*. London: Falmer.

Gardner, H. (1983). *Frames of mind: The theory of multiple intelligences*. New York: Basic Books.

Goleman, D. (1995). *Emotional intelligence*. New York: Bantam.

Hawkins, J. D., Catalano, R. F., & Miller, J. Y. (1992). Risk and protective factors for alcohol and other drug problems. *Psychological Bulletin, 112*(1), 64-105.

Henderson, N., & Milstein, M. M. (1996). *Resiliency in schools: Making it happen for students and educators*. Thousand Oaks, CA: Corwin.

Hesselbein, F., Goldsmith, M., Beckhard, R., & Schubert, R. F. (Eds.). (1998). *The community of the future*. San Francisco: Jossey-Bass.

Higgins, G. O. (1994). *Resilient adults: Overcoming a cruel past*. San Francisco: Jossey-Bass.

Higgins, R. (1985). *Psychological resilience and the capacity for intimacy: How the wounded might "love well."* Unpublished doctoral dissertation, Harvard University, Cambridge, MA.

Hord, S. M., Rutherford, W. L., Huling-Austin, L., & Hall, G. E. (1987). *Taking charge of change*. Alexandria, VA: Association for Supervision and Curriculum Development.

Huberman, M., & Miles, M. (1984). *Innovation up close*. New York: Plenum.

Johnson, D. W., & Johnson, F. P. (1991). *Joining together* (4th ed.). Englewood Cliffs, NJ: Prentice Hall.

Kretzmann, J. P., & McKnight, J. L. (1993). *Building communities from the inside out*. Chicago: ACTA.

Krovetz, M. L. (1999). *Fostering resiliency: Expecting all students to use their minds and hearts well*. Thousand Oaks, CA: Corwin.

Krueger, R. A. (1994). *Focus groups: A practical guide for applied research* (2nd ed.). Thousand Oaks, CA: Sage.

Lawson, H., & Briar-Lawson, K. (1997). *Connecting the dots: Progress toward the integration of school reform, school-linked services, parent involvement and community schools*. Oxford, OH: Danforth Foundation and Institute of Educational Renewal at Miami University.

Leffert, N., Benson, P. L., & Roehlkepartain, J. L. (1997). *Starting out right: Developmental assets for children*. San Francisco, Jossey-Bass.

Lickona, T. (1991). *Educating for character*. New York: Bantam.

McLaughlin, M. W., Irby, M. A., & Langman, J. (1994). *Urban sanctuaries*. San Francisco: Jossey-Bass

Miles, M. (1987, April). *Practical guidelines for school administrators: How to get there*. Paper presented at the annual Meeting of American Educational Research Association.

Milstein, M. M. (1993). *Restructuring schools: Doing it right*. Newbury Park, CA: Corwin.

Mycek, S. (1998, October). Heritage of health: Charleston's lessons for the nation. *Trustee*, pp. 8-13.

Napier, R. W., & Gershenfeld, M. K. (1993). *Groups: Theory and experience* (5th ed.). Boston: Houghton Mifflin.

National Commission on Excellence in Education. (1983). *A nation at risk*. Washington, DC: Author.

National Network for Family Resiliency. (1997). Communities in Schools, Charlotte, N.C. (site visit summary). http://www.exnet.iastate.edu/Pages?communications/Resiliency/cis.html

Orwell, G. (1949). *1984*. New York: Signet.

Owens, R. G. (1991). *Organizational behavior in education* (4th ed.). Englewood Cliffs, NJ: Prentice Hall.

Pascale, P. (1990). *Managing the edge*. New York: Touchstone.

Peters, T. J., & Waterman, R. H., Jr. (1982). *In search of excellence*. New York: Warner.

Pipher, M. (1996). *The shelter of each other: Rebuilding our families*. New York: Grosset/Putnam.

Richardson, G. E., Neiger, B. L., Jensen, S., & Krumpfer, K. L. (1990). The resiliency model. *Health Education, 21*(6), 33-39.

Roehlkepartain, E. C., & Benson, P. L. (1996). *Healthy communities-healthy schools*. Minneapolis, MN: Search Institute.

Rutter, M. (1989). Pathways from childhood to adult life. *Journal of Child Psychology and Psychiatry, 30*, 23-51.

Schmuck, R. A., & Runkel, P. J. (1994). *The handbook of organizational development in schools and colleges* (4th ed.). Prospect Heights, IL: Waveland Press.

Schorr, L. B. (1989). *Within our reach: Breaking the cycle of disadvantage*. New York: Anchor.

Schorr, L. B. (1997). *Common purpose: Strengthening families and neighborhoods to rebuild America*. New York: Doubleday.

Seago, L. (1997, Spring). C.U.R.E. for urban ills. *University of Memphis Alumni Magazine*, pp. 23-26.

Senge, P. (1990). *The fifth discipline.* New York: Doubleday.

Sergiovanni, T. J. (1990). *Value-added leadership.* San Diego, CA: Harcourt Brace Jovanovich.

Silverstein, S. (1974). *Where the sidewalk ends.* New York: HarperCollins.

Slavin, R. E., & Fashola, O. S. (1998). *Show me the evidence! Proven and promising programs for America's schools.* Thousand Oaks, CA: Corwin.

Starratt, R. J. (1996). *Transforming educational administration: Meaning, community, and excellence.* New York: McGraw-Hill.

Tannenbaum, R., & Schmidt. W. H. (1958, March-April). How to choose a leadership pattern. *Harvard Business Review, 36,* 95-101.

Taylor, M. (1995, June). *Fish in a stream: A metaphor for systemic and systematic school improvement.* Paper presented at the Region E TAC/Region 5 RTAC Title 1 regional Coordinating Council Meeting, Breckenridge, Colorado.

Tuckman, B. W. (1965).Developmental sequence in small groups. *Psychological Bulletin, 63,* 384-399.

Tyler, K. (1996). Collaboration: One community's. *Assets Magazine* (of Search Institute), pp. 8-11.

Warner, C. (1994). *Promoting your school.* Thousand Oaks, CA: Corwin.

Warner, C. (with Curry, M.). (1997). *Everybody's house—the schoolhouse.* Thousand Oaks, CA: Corwin.

Webster's collegiate dictionary (10th ed.). (1993). Springfield, MA: Merriam-Webster, Inc.

Werner, E. E., & Smith, R. S. (1992). *Overcoming the odds: High risk children from birth to adulthood.* New York: Cornell University Press.

Wheatley, M. J., & Kellner-Roger, M. (1998a). The paradox and promise of community. In F. Hesselbein, M. Goldsmith, R. Beckhard, & R. F. Schubert (Eds.), *The community of the future.* San Francisco: Jossey-Bass.

Wheatley, M. J., & Kellner-Roger, M. (1998b). Turning to one another: The possibilities of Y2K. In *Y2K citizen's action guide.* Minneapolis, MN: Utne Reader Books.

Wheatley, M. J., & Theobald, R. (1999). *Finding our role in resilient communities* [Videotape]. (Available from Northwest Regional Facilitators, East 525 Mission Avenue, Spokane, WA 99202)

Wolin, S. J., & Wolin, S. (1993). *The resilient self: How survivors of troubled families rise above adversity.* New York: Villard.

Yukl, G. (1998). *Leadership in organizations.* Upper Saddle River, NJ: Prentice Hall.

Index

CORWIN
PRESS

The Corwin Press logo—a raven striding across an open book—represents the happy union of courage and learning. We are a professional-level publisher of books and journals for K–12 educators, and we are committed to creating and providing resources that embody these qualities. Corwin's motto is "Success for All Learners."